Creighton
CSP, 1991

To Michelle,
With my prayerful
best wishes.
Charles J. Healey S.J.

# MODERN
# SPIRITUAL WRITERS

# MODERN SPIRITUAL WRITERS
## THEIR LEGACIES OF PRAYER

\*

Charles J. Healey, SJ

ALBA · HOUSE    NEW · YORK

SOCIETY OF ST. PAUL, 2187 VICTORY BLVD., STATEN ISLAND, NEW YORK 10314

*Library of Congress Cataloging-in-Publication Data*

Healey, Charles J.
    Modern spiritual writers : their legacies of prayer /
    by Charles J. Healey.
        p.    cm.
    Bibliography: p.
    ISBN 0-8189-0550-6
    1. Spirituality — Catholic Church — History.  2. Spirituality —
History.  3. Catholic Church — Doctrines — History.
  I. Title.
BX2350.65.H43     1989                89-30504
248'.092'2 — dc20                        CIP

Designed, printed and bound in the United States of
America by the Fathers and Brothers of the
Society of St. Paul, 2187 Victory Boulevard,
Staten Island, New York 10314, as part of their
communications apostolate.

**Printing Information:**

Current Printing - first digit     2  3  4  5  6  7  8  9  10  11  12

Year of Current Printing - first year shown
        1990     1991     1992     1993     1994     1995     1996

*DEDICATED*

*to*

**MY MOTHER**

*and*

*to the Memory of*

**MY FATHER**

# PREFACE

IN THE FOLLOWING CHAPTERS, the lives and writings of nine spiritual writers are treated. Although the choice of these nine authors has been somewhat arbitrary, all of them do fall within certain parameters. In the first place, all of them are now deceased. Secondly, each of them can be considered a modern writer. With the exception of John Henry Newman, all have lived and died in this present century. Finally, all of them are significant spiritual writers, although in some cases their reputation as writers is broader than this category. For example, Newman, C.S. Lewis, and Teilhard de Chardin have made significant contributions in other areas of scholarship.

The genesis of this book is found in courses I have taught over the years on modern spiritual writers. A certain variety of authors was found to be desirable, and this is reflected in the choice made for this book. Of the six Catholic writers, four are men (Newman, Marmion, Merton and Teilhard) and two are women (Dorothy Day and Caryll Houselander). The others include one Anglican (C.S. Lewis), one Lutheran (Dietrich Bonhoeffer) and one Jewish writer (Abraham Heschel).

It is hoped that these chapters will provide a helpful introduction to these spiritual writers. It often happens that someone would like to become better acquainted with the life and writings of a particular author, but is unsure about the best way to proceed. These essays seek to provide this guidance. Obviously, there is no substitution for the actual reading of the authors. But often some assistance and guidance can be helpful and even necessary. Thus the treatment of each of these authors seeks to serve as an incentive to the reader to explore their writings more fully, while at the same time providing guidance and focusing.

Karl Rahner, with his wide-ranging interests, found the lives and writings of Christian saints and mystics to be an excellent source for contemporary theological reflection. It seems to me that this can be extended to many modern spiritual writers who have made significant contributions to the larger community of faith with the account of their own experiences of God and the spiritual themes they have developed in their writings.

All authors are influenced in their writings to some degree by their own lives and experiences, but this seems to be especially true in the case of spiritual authors. Much of what they emphasize in their writings flows from their own experience of God and the movements of His grace in their lives. If we are to understand the thrust of their spiritual writings, then, it is important to recall the experience of God in their own lives. I have found that this can also be very beneficial to ourselves. For, as we reflect on their journeys of faith, we are often led by God's grace to reflect upon our own journeys.

With this in mind, the treatment of each spiritual writer begins with a look at the significant religious experiences that shaped his or her unique relationship with God. What is aimed at is not so much a sketch of their lives, but an understanding of the significant events and experiences that influenced their spiritual themes and the general thrust of their religious writings. This is followed by an investigation of the main characteristics and themes of their

spirituality as found in their writings. Finally, there is gener-
ally a discussion of their reflections on prayer, because for all
of them prayer was a constant and extremely significant
aspect of their spirituality. Their insights on prayer can be
particularly helpful and timely since there is such a renewed
interest on the part of so many regarding prayer.

The chapters have been arranged according to the year
of the authors' deaths, beginning with those closest to us in
time. Thus, the first chapter treats Dorothy Day who died in
1980 while the last chapter deals with Cardinal Newman
who died in 1890. Each chapter is a complete unity in itself
so the reader is free to read them in whatever order is
desired. Suggestions for further readings for each writer are
included at the end.

Although there are great differences in each of the
authors by way of backgrounds, temperaments, individual
experiences and vocations, there are also many striking
similarities in the spiritual themes they present in their
writings. There is, for example, the strong sense of God's
reality that each of them expresses so powerfully. Along
with this is the conviction of God's importance in our lives
and the priority that must be given to Him. Abraham
Heschel sums it up with the expression, "God is of no importance unless He is of supreme importance." For Thomas
Merton, the expression "God alone" always spoke to the
very depths in him. There is also the strong conviction of
God working powerfully and personally in their lives. For
Dorothy Day it was marked by a sense of God's haunting
presence in her life and a sense of her own particular mission. For Newman, it was a sense of God's loving providence
that he expressed so well in his beloved poem, "Lead, Kindly
Light."

The centrality of Christ is another common theme that
looms large. Although it may be expressed in different

terms and with different emphases, it is often central to their spirituality. For Marmion, it is Christ who is "the life of the soul." Dorothy Day will stress the Mystical Body of Christ and our union with one another in Him. Caryll Houselander's basic message focuses on the challenge to see Christ in everyone and live accordingly. Teilhard de Chardin identifies the Omega Point, the final point of all human effort and progress, with the Risen Christ.

As the title of the book indicates, their reflections on prayer will be highlighted. All of the authors were convinced that a life of prayer was central and essential to any relationship with God. Prayer played an important and crucial part in their own lives, and this significance is reflected in their writings. Each of them has a particular legacy to share, and we are richer for it.

Although all of these spiritual writers were extraordinary men and women who were gifted in many ways, it is interesting to note the sense of reality and practicality that is found in their writings. Over and over we find them stressing that a person's relationship with God and one's life of faith and prayer must be integrated with one's ordinary, daily life. God is to be found and embraced in the ordinary events of one's life. They seek to bring together the reality of God and the reality of the everyday experiences of the individual person.

Finally, since each of these chapters focuses on a particular author and his or her writings, some passages from their works are given to assist in the exposition of their thought and to provide a flavor of their particular style. But again, there is no substitute for going directly to their writings. It is my hope that this book will help to make each of these authors more alive to the reader, who in turn may be helped in his or her own journey in faith to draw closer to God and to penetrate the mystery of His love in one's own life.

# ACKNOWLEDGMENTS

Excerpts from *The Seven Storey Mountain* by Thomas Merton, copyright 1948 by Harcourt Brace Jovanovich, Inc., renewed 1976 by the Trustees of the Merton Legacy Trust. Reprinted by permission of Harcourt Brace Jovanovich, Inc.

Excerpts from *Life Together* by Dietrich Bonhoeffer, copyright 1954 by Harper & Row, Publishers, Inc. Reprinted by permission of the publisher.

Excerpts from *The Long Loneliness* by Dorothy Day, copyright 1952 by Harper & Row, Publishers, Inc. Reprinted by permission of the publisher.

Excerpts from *The Life and Death of Dietrich Bonhoeffer* by Mary Bosanquet, copyright 1968 by Mary Bosanquet. Reprinted by permission of Harper & Row, Publishers, Inc.

Excerpts from *Man is Not Alone* by Abraham Joshua Heschel, copyright 1951 by Abraham Joshua Heschel, renewed 1979 by Sylvia Heschel. Reprinted by permission of Farrar, Straus and Giroux, Inc.

Excerpts from *God in Search of Man* by Abraham Joshua Heschel, copyright 1955 by Abraham Joshua Heschel, renewed 1983 by Sylvia Heschel. Reprinted by permission of Farrar, Straus and Giroux, Inc.

# CONTENTS

# THEIR LEGACIES OF PRAYER

# Dorothy
# DAY (1897-1980)

DOROTHY DAY's name has become synonymous
with the Catholic Worker apostolate, for she was intimately
connected with this significant movement in the American
Catholic Church since its beginning in 1932. God blessed
her with a long and fruitful life — a life that was marked by a
dedication to voluntary poverty and the service of the poor.
Perhaps nothing stands out so forcibly in her life as her
constancy and faithfulness. She steadfastly lived and worked
within the Church and she served the poor with heroic
constancy and fidelity.

Writing always played a large part in her life. She never
considered herself a scholarly writer and never attempted to
approach her subjects in a systematic way. But she was a
respected journalist who could write well about her own
experiences in life and the people, events and issues connected with her active life and work. As we consider her life
and writings, we will look first at her own experience of God,
particularly during her years of searching; secondly, at some
general characteristics of her spirituality; and, finally, some
particular aspects of her legacy of prayer.

# *I*

Since Dorothy Day has written two autobiographical works, *From Union Square to Rome* and *The Long Loneliness*, we have a good deal of information about her spiritual odyssey and the events that led to her conversion to Catholicism. As we focus on the role of prayer in her life, it will be helpful to look at some of the significant influences and experiences that marked her relationship with God during the years of her searching.

The theme of being pursued by God was always a striking and moving one for Dorothy Day. At the beginning of *The Long Loneliness* she writes simply: " 'All my life I have been haunted by God,' as Kiriloff said in *The Possessed*."[1] As she looked back upon her life, she often noted the presence of a religious sentiment within her that struggled to exert itself. Her own experience in this regard led her to the conviction that every person has a basic tendency toward God. In this connection we might note that more than once she mentions how moved she was as a young woman when she first heard Eugene O'Neill recite Francis Thompson's poem, "The Hound of Heaven," in a tavern in Greenwich Village where she would meet frequently with friends after a rehearsal or performance that took place at the Providencetown Playhouse. Years later she recalled its effects as she wrote: "The idea of this pursuit of the Hound of Heaven fascinated me. The recurrence of it, the inevitableness of the outcome made me feel that sooner or later I would have to pause in the mad rush of living and remember my first beginning and my last end."[2]

Dorothy Day describes the first part of her life as a struggle to find meaning and purpose, and something to which she could dedicate herself: "The first twenty-five years were floundering, years of joy and sorrow, it is true, but certainly with a sense of that insecurity one hears so much about these days. I did not know in what I believed, though I tried to serve a cause."[3]

During these years, religion played a limited role, although seeds were planted and at times the religious sense within her struggled to assert itself. During these years, too, she never fully suppressed an attraction to prayer and worship. For example, she was deeply moved as a young girl when she ran in on a neighbor unexpectedly and found her praying on her knees. The example of someone praying in a hidden, simple way touched her deeply and years later she wrote: "And I felt a warmth of love towards Mrs. Barrett that I have never forgotten, a feeling of gratitude and happiness that still warms my heart when I remember her. She had God and there was beauty and joy in her life."[4] She also tells us that the Psalms became a part of her childhood through her attendance for a period at an Episcopal church in New York City. She grew to love the Psalms and learned many of them by heart. This love of the Psalms would never leave her, and they became an outlet for many of the emotions she would experience in her life. Psalms of praise had a particular attraction for her.

It was to the Psalms that she turned for comfort and solace when she took part in a hunger strike during her first prison experience. She was a young woman of eighteen at the time and had gone to Washington to picket the White House with the Suffragists. Their picketing in protest of the treatment given in prison to other Suffragists led to their own imprisonment and their decision to go on a hunger strike until their demands were met for the rights of political prisoners. The solitary confinement and the fast took their toll on her, and she was plunged into a deep sense of discouragement and desolation. As she reflected on the desolation of poverty, destitution, sickness and sin, she seemed to lose all feeling of her own identity. Later she would write powerfully of her identification with those around her in prison, for this experience had left an indelible impression upon her.

She had asked for the Bible early in her imprisonment and it was brought to her on the fourth day. Although she clung to the words of comfort in the Bible, and read and pondered in a special way the words of the Psalms, she tells us that she did so with some reluctance. She did not want to go to God in defeat and sorrow and she did not want to depend on Him. She tried to persuade herself that she was reading for literary enjoyment, "but the words kept echoing in my heart. I prayed and did not know that I prayed."[5]

This was part of the conflict that had grown acute in her life during her two years of college in Chicago and continued during the years she worked as a journalist in New York City. She had become acutely conscious of class warfare and social injustice, and she felt religion would impede her work. These social interests and religion seemed irreconcilable, and for her the choice was clear:

> I felt at the time that religion would impede my work. I wanted to have nothing to do with the religion of those whom I saw all around me. I felt that I must turn from it as from a drug. I felt it indeed to be an opiate of the people and not a very attractive one, so I hardened my heart. It was a conscious and deliberate process.[6]

And yet the religious sentiment in her continued to struggle to assert itself from time to time. The attraction to worship and ritual remained strong. For example, she tells us that on many a morning after sitting all night in a tavern or coming from balls at Webster Hall, she went to an early Mass at St. Joseph's Church on Sixth Avenue. She knelt in the back of the church not knowing what was going on at the altar but warmed and comforted by the kneeling people and the atmosphere. Also during the year of her training as a nurse, she accompanied her Catholic companion at the hospital to Mass every Sunday morning. In recalling this she writes: "One thing I was sure of and that was that these fellow workers and I were performing an act of worship. I felt that it was necessary for man to worship, that he was most truly himself when engaged in that act."[7]

Part Two of her autobiography, *The Long Loneliness*, is entitled, "Natural Happiness." Dorothy Day always felt that it was through a human love that she came to know and love God.[8] She entered into a common-law marriage with a man named Forster, and they lived in a little house along the beach on Staten Island. It was a happy time for her in many ways, and a time of much growth. There was time for writing and study amidst the beauties of nature, and there were many friends with whom she could share her interests. However, her growing concern with religion and her movement towards a complete faith brought problems with Forster. He was an anarchist who was so adamantly opposed to any religion that she realized he would have nothing to do with her if she embraced religion. She writes of their relationship: "But it was impossible to talk about religion or faith to him. A wall immediately separated us. The very love of nature, and the study of her secrets which was bringing me to faith, cut Forster off from religion."[9]

During this period of waiting, Dorothy Day was surprised to find herself beginning to pray frequently. In walks to the village she would pray the rosary a friend had given her years earlier. She began to attend Mass regularly on Sunday mornings and she would pray as she walked along the beach. She did not fully understand this attraction to prayer and the delight she found in it, but she quietly accepted the mystery of God working within her. In this quiet, somewhat contemplative atmosphere she also read some solid spiritual classics. In addition to the Bible, she read the *Imitation of Christ*, the writings of St. Augustine, Teresa of Avila, John of the Cross and others. She found the *Imitation of Christ* particularly helpful and the reading of Dostoevsky's novels continued to be a profound religious experience for her.

It was a time, too, for waiting for the birth of her daughter Tamar Teresa. When the child was born, she was intent on having her baptized, and she made arrangement for the baptism through a nun she had met, Sister Aloysia. The nun also gave instructions to Dorothy Day herself and moved her closer to her own conversion to Catholicism. Yet she waited, for she knew it would be a difficult and costly decision. First, she realized only too clearly that it would lead to a break with Forster, and the loss of his love and companionship would not be easy. She knew that she and the child would be alone, and she did not want to be alone. Secondly, the conflict between religion and her strong social consciousness was not fully resolved at this time. She writes of this struggle: "I had become convinced that I would become a Catholic; yet I felt I was betraying the class to which I belonged, the workers, the poor of the world, with whom Christ spent His life."[10]

She sought out a priest and followed his advice of waiting. In the time of waiting and seeking, she was most likely consoled by the words of Pascal, for she quotes them while writing about this period: "Thou wouldst not seek Him if thou hadst not already found Him."[11]

The waiting came to an end in December, 1927. Dorothy Day entered the Catholic Church and received the sacraments of Baptism, Penance, and Holy Eucharist on the same day. For her, however, it was not a day of consolation and joy, and there was no conviction that what she was doing was right. It was something she had to do. She tells us that she never regretted the step she took in becoming a Catholic, but the struggle continued during the first year and she found little joy in her faith. She received the sacrament of Confirmation a year after she became a Catholic, and this occasion found her much more settled and at peace. It was a joyous occasion for her and she writes: "It was only then that the feeling of uncertainty left me, never again to return praise God."[12]

Dorothy Day was thirty years old when she became a Catholic in 1927. Five years would pass before her meeting with Peter Maurin and their launching of the Catholic Worker movement. These five years continued to be years of spiritual growth and the deepening of her spirit of faith and prayer. But they also continued to be years of searching. She was seeking to integrate her faith with her social interest and deeply felt human concerns. Peter Maurin would prove to be the catalyst through whom she would find the inspiration, cause and movement to which she could dedicate herself generously and faithfully over the course of many, many years. From its beginning in 1932, Dorothy Day would be intimately connected with the Catholic Worker movement, and was really its heart and inspiration for countless people.[13]

## *II*

Now that we have seen the significant experiences and influences in Dorothy Day's spiritual odyssey and her long road to Catholicism, we are in a better position to reflect upon some of the main aspects of her spirituality.

There was, first of all, a very strong sense of mission. Of course, this came to focus on her activities in the Catholic Worker movement. But long before this she was aware of a haunting sense of mission that she felt had to be fulfilled in some way. She writes on her reaction to the poverty she encountered as a young woman in New York City: "And yet as I walked the streets back in 1917 I wanted to go and live among these surroundings; in some mysterious way I felt that I would never be freed from this burden of loneliness and sorrow unless I did."[14]   She also writes in a similar vein: "Through all my daily life, in those I came in contact with, in the things I read and heard, I felt that sense of being followed, of being desired; a sense of hope and expectation."[15]   For many years this sense of mission was only expressed in such vague and searching terms as the above. What Dorothy Day sought in her life after her conversion was some kind of a synthesis — a synthesis of her strong religious faith that had come to the fore, and her deep social interests and radical concerns.

It was Peter Maurin who provided this synthesis and sense of mission when they met five years after she had become a Catholic. She felt he had provided her with "a way of life and instruction" and for this she was always deeply grateful. She describes very clearly this sense of mission Peter Maurin had the ability to inspire in others. It became deeply engrained in her life and vision:

> Peter made you feel a sense of his mission as soon as you met him. He did not begin by tearing down, or by painting so intense a picture of misery and injustice that you burned to change the world. Instead, he aroused in you a sense of your own capacities for

> work, for accomplishment. He made you feel that
> you and all men had great and generous hearts with
> which to love God. If you once recognized this fact in
> yourself you would expect and find it in others.
> "The art of human contacts," Peter called it happily.
> But it was seeing Christ in others, loving the Christ
> you saw in others. Greater than this, it was having
> faith in the Christ in others without being able to see
> Him. Blessed is he that believes without seeing.[16]

Dorothy Day's pervading sense of trust in God's providence was closely connected with this strong sense of mission. Shortly after her conversion, her first spiritual director, Fr. Joseph McSorley, gave her a copy of De Caussade's *Abandonment to Divine Providence*. It was a book that spoke to her powerfully and influenced her deeply. It is interesting to note in this connection that it was Fr. McSorley who advised her to go and speak wherever she was invited. She took this advice, sensing that God was leading her in these invitations. For years she would travel by bus to speak about her work, to encourage and to give witness.

Peter Maurin set the stage for this sense of trust in God's providence that so marked the Catholic Worker movement when he told Dorothy Day at the time they first discussed starting a newspaper: "In the history of the saints, capital was raised by prayer. God sends you what you need when you need it. You will be able to pay the printer, just read the lives of the saints."[17] This sense of trust in God's providence was put into practice over and over again throughout the years, as the Catholic Worker movement expanded its activities. There was the strong trust that God would provide if they gave themselves to Him completely.[18]

Another major characteristic of Dorothy Day's spirituality was the primacy that she gave to the basic gospel message of love of neighbor in her own life and the Catholic Worker movement. In her mind there was no doubt that we are our brother's keeper and should act accordingly. She sought to serve the poor in a spirit of voluntary poverty and gave herself to them in selfless love. Her words on this subject are important, but what is far more important is the witness she herself gave year after year. The words take on greater meaning and force when seen in the light of her example. Her aim and the aim of the Catholic Worker movement was to manifest this love in action on all levels of life.

Realist that she was, she knew that at times this active love could be demanding and discouraging. It called for faith and patience and unselfishness. She never tired of recalling the words of Fr. Zossima in Dostoevsky's novel, *The Brothers Karamazov.* Since these words sum up so much of her spirit and the motivating force in her life, it will be helpful to recall them here:

> . . . love in action is a harsh and dreadful thing compared with love in dreams. Love in dreams is greedy for immediate action, rapidly performed and in the sight of all. Men will even give their lives if only the ordeal does not last long but is soon over, with all looking on and applauding as though on the stage. But active love is labor and fortitude, and for some people too perhaps a complete science. But I predict that just when you see with horror that in spite of all your efforts you are getting further from your goal, instead of nearer to it — at that very moment I predict that you will reach it and behold clearly the miraculous power of the Lord who has been all the time loving and mysteriously guiding you.[19]

Thus for Dorothy Day, there was an intimate relationship between knowing and loving the God she served and recognizing Him and serving Him in the poor and the outcast. She experienced this in her own life and in her relationship with God. Recalling another story from *The Brothers Karamazov* that focused on the effects of a poor woman giving away an onion, Dorothy Day reflected: "Sometimes in thinking and wondering at God's goodness to me I have thought that it was because I gave away an onion. Because I sincerely loved His poor He taught me to know Him. And when I think of the little I ever did, I am filled with hope and love for all those others devoted to the cause of social justice."[20]   The corporal and spiritual works of mercy were at the heart of all the activity of the Catholic Worker movement.

In light of her conviction of the presence of Christ in others, it is not surprising to find Dorothy Day stressing so strongly in her writings the doctrine of the Mystical Body of Christ. In fact, we can say that the Catholic Worker movement is based on the teaching of the Gospels and the doctrine of the Mystical Body of Christ. The realization of our unity in Christ and the value of community took on great importance in her life and writings. For her, community was the answer to the long loneliness:

> We cannot love God unless we love each other, and to love we must know each other. We know Him in the breaking of bread, and we know each other in the breaking of bread, and we are not alone any more. Heaven is a banquet and life is a banquet, too, even with a crust, where there is companionship.

> We have all known the long loneliness and we have learned that the only solution is love and that love comes with community.[21]

This sense of being united in the Mystical Body manifested itself in many ways — for example, in the sensitive and reflective way she wrote about various people. There are some very vivid and poignant portraits of people who crossed her life in a significant way over the course of the years. Even though many of the persons she wrote about were no longer alive, she conveyed a sense of union with them. For example, the pages where she speaks about Rayna Prohme are very poignant as she recognizes her basic goodness and joyful spirit. Similarly, her description of the Bodenheims, her contact with them, and their tragic deaths, are very moving. As she describes these and other people, she seems to be united with them in memory and prayer.[22]

# *III*

Let us look more closely now at some of the particular aspects of Dorothy Day's prayer. It should be clear from what we have seen already that prayer was certainly an important part of her life. It should be helpful now to highlight some of the emphases that emerge from her witness of the value of prayer in her daily life.

As noted earlier, Dorothy Day was not a spiritual writer who treated the subject of prayer in any systematic way. But she could write well about her own experiences and the important persons and events in her life. She recognized, too, the close connection that existed in her life between her prayer and the writing which occupied a good deal of her time:

> I shall meditate as I have been accustomed, in the
> little Italian Church in Twelfth Street, by the side of
> the open window, looking out at the plants growing

on the roof, the sweet corn, the boxes of herbs, the
geraniums in bright bloom, and I shall rest happy in
the presence of Christ on the altar, and then I shall
come home and I shall write as Pére Graty advises,
and try to catch some of these things that happen to
bring me nearer to God, to catch them and put them
down on paper.

It is something I have wanted to do, which I have
done sketchily for some years. Usually I have kept a
notebook only when I am sad and need to work
myself out of my sadness. Now I shall do it as a duty
performed joyfully for God.

And because I am a woman involved in practical
cares, I cannot give the first half of the day to these
things, but must meditate when I can, early in the
morning and on the fly during the day. Not in the
privacy of a study — but here, there and everywhere
— at the kitchen table, on the train, on the ferry, on
my way to and from appointments and even while
making supper or putting Teresa to bed.[23]

Dorothy Day's prayer itself could be characterized as
existential in the sense that she was constantly aware of the
Lord's presence in her life through her yearning, her joys,
her desolations, her daily activities and contacts with others.
She was faithful to this experience as she grew to interpret
under God's grace its specific meaning in her life.

She had a normal and natural way of incorporating
prayer into her life. There was nothing artificial about her
prayer nor was it something that was relegated to the private
sphere. It was part of her daily life and it required no
defense or apology. She was always very moved when she
saw the natural place that prayer played in the life of a

person. She would frequently note in her writings the quiet, natural witness others gave of prayer.[24]

Since there were so many demands on her time, and so little privacy given the nature of her work and the voluntary poverty of the Catholic Worker movement, she had to pray when and how she could. It is interesting to note how often she speaks about some aspect of prayer while writing about some of her brief experiences in jail on behalf of various causes. Again she was always moved at the sight of others praying and she would not hesitate to pray in the presence of others, quietly giving witness to the importance and significance of prayer in her life even in these circumstances.

Prayer in common at various times of the day was also a normal and regular part of life at the House of Hospitality where Dorothy Day lived and worked. For example, the rosary was recited at noontime in the common reading room, and Compline was prayed together in the evening. When word came of Peter Maurin's death, prayer was the first response of her and of those with her at the time: "When I hung up the receiver, Bill suggested we say Vespers of the Office of the Dead for Peter. So we knelt there in the farm living room and prayed those beautiful psalms that are balm to the sore heart."[25]

Her prayer, then, was incorporated and fused into her daily life. This, of course, brings us to the question of the relationship between contemplation (prayer) and action. It is interesting to see how Dorothy Day dealt with the connection between her relationship with God and her life of prayer, and her constant and continuous activity. This is a tension that evolves in the life of every person who is serious about both prayer and apostolic work.

There was no question of the importance for Dorothy Day of a life of service and apostolic work for the building up of God's Kingdom. Her meeting with Peter Maurin and their founding of the Catholic Worker movement gave a clear focus to her strong sense of mission, and she gave herself to the works of mercy and of justice with great generosity and constancy. She seemed to sense that this was her vocation under God's grace, for she writes:

> We have always acknowledged the primacy of the spiritual, and to have undertaken a life of silence, manual labor and prayer might have been the better way. But I do not know. God gives us our tempera-ments, and in spite of my pacifism, it is natural for me to stand my ground, to continue in what actually amounts to a class war, using such weapons as the works of mercy for immediate means to show our love and to alleviate suffering.[26]

Although she was convinced of the importance of both prayer and apostolic work in her life, Dorothy Day also recognized the challenge that was ever present to integrate both of these aspects in a productive and balanced way. In general, she was able to maintain a healthy balance, al-though, as might be expected, she herself was never fully satisfied.

She knew well that her life was a very active one. There was much for her to do and others made many demands on her time and energy. But she had no illusions about her need for prayer and other spiritual activities if her apostolic work was to be nourished and she was to persevere patiently and in a spirit of hope. Discouragement was a constant temptation. Thus she valued and made use of the traditional means of nourishing one's life in the Spirit. The daily

Eucharist had first place in her spiritual life. She began to attend daily Mass not too long after her conversion and this always remained the important source of prayer and worship for her. There was also the reading of Scripture, meditation, daily rosary, and the recitation of parts of the Divine Office.

Among other means she used to nourish her faith and her prayer life, the continual reading of spiritual books played a strong part. It is clear from her columns "On Pilgrimage" and from her other writings that she was constantly reading books that would be helpful to her spiritual life. We have seen how helpful she found the reading of the many classical spiritual authors before and after her conversion. This practice of spiritual reading became a regular and beneficial part of her life, and she would read whenever she could. Her frequent journeys by bus afforded her special opportunities for this.

The role of retreats is also stressed in her writings. She realized she needed time on occasions to concentrate on her relationship with God, as well as time for some solitude and prayer. From time to time she organized retreats and days of recollection for herself and her associates at the Catholic Worker. She writes in this connection: "It is not only for others that I must have these retreats. It is because I too am hungry and thirsty for the bread of the strong. I too must nourish myself to do the work I have undertaken; I too must drink at these springs so that I may not be an empty cistern and unable to help others."[27]

Dorothy Day was also careful to make use of good spiritual directors and confessors, and she was open and responsive to their advice and suggestions. As we have seen, Joseph McSorley was her first spiritual director, and she often paid tribute to the help he gave to her. She also had the good common sense to know when she wasn't receiving good advice. On one occasion, a confessor apparently did not understand her and her work, and she was prudent enough to choose someone else.

A particular source of concern for her in connection with the relationship between prayer and action was the need she expressed for a daily program. Often in her writings, we find her commenting on the necessity of having some daily program for the time allotted to her prayer and spiritual activities. Given the nature of her work and its continued activity and demands, it is not surprising that this would be a constant concern.[28]   Realist that she was, she knew that a program or structure is not an end in itself, but a means to further her union with God. After carefully considering a daily program, she writes on one occasion: "The thing to remember is not to read so much or talk so much about God, but to talk to God."[29]   Then linking her prayer to her everyday life, she adds that the most important aspect of all is to practice the presence of God and to be gentle and charitable in thought, word and deed.

Prayer for Dorothy Day also provided a great deal of support and strength. Again this should be seen in light of her demanding work which exposed her continually to a side of life that was often grim and depressing. It is not surprising that at times discouragement set in, but in these moments prayer was a great aid. It helped her to restore a balance and perspective in her life. For example, after a particularly trying period, she writes:

> And the after effects of last night's and this morning's heavy praying have been peace and joy and strength and thanksgiving, and a great deal of humility too, at being so weak that God had to send me consolation to prepare me for the next trial.

> I should know by this time that just because I *feel* that
> everything is useless and going to pieces and badly
> done and futile, it is not really that way at all. Every-
> thing is all right. It is in the hands of God. Let us
> abandon everything to Divine Providence.[30]

Finally, she related the need for prayer to the events at
hand. She ends a book that collects her "On Pilgrimage"
articles of the 1960's with reflections on a charismatic prayer
meeting she attended. Writing just after news broke of
atrocities that were committed during the Vietnam War, she
says:

> The need for prayer! All those at that meeting were
> going out to a hostile world, a world of such horrors
> just this week that it is hard to see how happiness can
> ever come to us again. . . . We must do penance for
> what we have done to our brothers. We are our
> brother's keeper.
>
> But meanwhile in this hushed room there was
> prayer, for strength to know and to love and to find
> out what to do and set our hands to useful work that
> will contribute to peace, not to war.
>
> Love is the measure by which we will be judged.[31]

\*   \*   \*   \*   \*   \*   \*

Dorothy Day's strong witness of a life of service to the
poor and the prophetic role she has played in the Catholic
Church in the mid-twentieth century has long been recognized. *America* magazine celebrated her 75th birthday in
November, 1972, with a special issue dedicated to her and
the Catholic Worker movement. Her unique contributions

to the Church and to society were clearly noted: "By now, if one had to choose a single individual to symbolize the best in the aspiration and action of the American Catholic community during the last forty years, that one person would surely be Dorothy Day."[32]

Perhaps what stands out most clearly in her life is the witness she has given in many things. She has been a witness to a deep faith in God and an abiding spirit of prayer; to a life of voluntary poverty and the service of the poor; to a steadfastness and constancy in laboring to build up God's Kingdom here on earth; to the integrating and living out of the two great commandments, love of God and love of neighbor. As the *America* issue stressed, she has grasped with enormous force and clarity the essentials of the Christian life, and through the witness of her life and labors she never fails to remind us of them. For all this we are much richer. In the Lord's service, Dorothy Day of the Catholic Worker movement was indeed a good and faithful Catholic and worker.

---

1 Dorothy Day, *The Long Loneliness* (New York: Curtis Books, 1972), p. 10. This work was first published in 1952.

2 *Ibid.*, p. 96.

3 *Ibid.*, p. 9.

4 Dorothy Day, *From Union Square to Rome* (Maryland, Preservation of the Faith Press, 1938), p. 24. Cf. also *The Long Loneliness*, p. 26.

5 *The Long Loneliness*, p. 92.

6 *Ibid.*, p. 48.

7 *Ibid.*, p. 107.

8 She writes: "It was because through a whole love, both physical and spiritual, I came to know God." *Ibid.*, p. 160.

9 *Ibid.*, p. 153. She also writes: "His ardent love of creation brought me to the Creator of all things, but when I cried out to him, 'How can there be no God when there are all these beautiful things,' he turned from me uneasily and complained that I was never satisfied." *Ibid.*

10 *Ibid.*, p. 165.

11 Quoted in *The Long Loneliness*, p. 159.

12  *From Union Square to Rome*, p. 142.
13  Dorothy Day wrote a great deal about the Catholic Worker movement and its purpose, philosophy, ideals, etc. See, for example, her book *Loaves and Fishes* (New York: Curtis Books, 1972; first published in 1963). See also William D. Miller's *A Harsh and Dreadful Love: Dorothy Day and the Catholic Worker movement* (New York: Liveright, 1973).
14  *The Long Loneliness*, p. 58.
15  *From Union Square to Rome*, p. 142.
16  *The Long Loneliness*, pp. 195-196.
17  *Ibid.*, p. 197.
18  Again it is interesting to note that at the beginning of *The Long Loneliness*, Dorothy Day gives this quote from the writings of Mary Ward, an English nun of the early 17th century: "I think, dear child, the trouble and the long loneliness you hear me speak of is not far from me, which wherever it is, happy success will follow. . . . The pain is great, but very endurable because He who lays on the burden also carries it." p. 6.
19  F. Dostoevsky, *The Brothers Karamazov*, bk. 2, ch. 4. Dorothy Day herself writes in summing up the significance of the Catholic Worker movement: "But the final work is love. At times it has been, in the words of Father Zossima, a harsh and dreadful thing, and our very faith in love has been tried through fire." *The Long Loneliness*, p. 317.
20  *From Union Square to Rome*, p. 9. In seeking to answer the question, "How can you see Christ in people," Dorothy Day writes: "It is an act of love resulting from an act of faith. It is an act of hope that we can awaken the same acts in their hearts too with the help of God and the works of mercy. . . ." cf. *On Pilgrimage: the Sixties* (New York: Curtis Books, 1972), p. 168.
21  *The Long Loneliness*, pp. 317-318. She also writes: "The only answer in this life to the loneliness we are all bound to feel is community, the living together, working together, sharing together, loving God and loving our brother, and living close to him in community so we can show our love for Him." *Ibid.*, p. 272.
22  For her remarks about Rayna Prohme, see *The Long Loneliness*, pp. 52-55; for the Bodenheims, see *Loaves and Fishes*, pp. 151-155.
23  Dorothy Day, *House of Hospitality* (New York: Sheed & Ward, 1939), pp. 2-3.
24  Cf. for example her description of Peter Maurin praying in *Loaves and Fishes*, p. 14.
25  *The Long Loneliness*, p. 311.
26  *Ibid.*, p. 206.
27  *Ibid.*, p. 294.
28  The following indicates the seriousness with which she took the need of prayer in her daily life and the time she gave to it. "How much time is consciously spent in prayer? Three-quarters of an hour in the morning at Mass; Rosary and visit, one half hour. Night prayer, one half hour. Say, two hours all told.

Spiritual reading one or two hours. Sleep seven hours, which leaves thirteen hours of activity. Too much." From *House of Hospitality*, pp. 100-101.

29 *Ibid.*, p. 132.

30 *House of Hospitality*, pp. 97-98. Dorothy Day writes elsewhere: "The frustrations that we experience are exercises in faith and hope which are supernatural virtues. With prayer, one can go on cheerfully and even happily. Without prayer, how grim a journey!" *Loaves and Fishes*, p. 200.

31 *On Pilgrimage: The Sixties*, p. 383.

32 *America* (Nov. 11, 1972), p. 378. This introductory editorial also adds: "She has persevered in faith, hope and charity for forty years of a pilgrimage that must often enough seemed to be winding through a wilderness."

# Abraham Joshua
# HESCHEL (1907-1972)

ABRAHAM JOSHUA HESCHEL was remarkable in many ways. He was a man of strong faith with deep roots in his Jewish heritage. He was a renowned scholar who made significant contributions in biblical, rabbinic, medieval philosophic, Hasidic and mystical thought. He was a gifted writer with a poetic, lofty and moving style. Although his roots were sunk deeply in traditional thought and piety, he was a man of his time, passionately concerned with contemporary issues and problems.[1] Profoundly Jewish and deeply committed to his Jewish faith, he was also a man who uniquely belonged to the entire American religious community.[2]

For Jews, Heschel's message is a constant call to be faithful to the very best in their religious tradition. For Christians and others, his life, his vision and his writings can be a rich source of inspiration as they seek to grow and be nourished in the practice of their own faith. As an example of his wide ecumenical influence, we might recall Pope Paul VI's citation from Heschel's *God in Search of Man* in an address to a general audience that was gathered at the Vatican. Toward the end of his remarks on the nature of one's quest for God, he cited a familiar theme of Heschel's and reminded his hearers that "even before we have moved in search of God, God has come in search of us."[3]

The Second Vatican Council recognized that the spiritual patrimony common to Christians and Jews was great and sought "to foster and recommend that mutual understanding and respect which is the fruit above all of biblical and theological studies, and of brotherly dialogue."[4]   Following this lead, Christians will have to go far to find one who surpasses Abraham Heschel in the breadth and depth of the witness he provides in his own Jewish tradition through his life and writings.

Heschel's conviction of the importance of prayer stands out clearly throughout his writings. The reality of God in our lives and our corresponding response were his constant themes. There is also his own living faith that shines through his remarks on prayer and reflects a man of prayer himself.

He does not write about prayer in any systematic way. He addresses himself to the subject on various occasions in various ways and seemingly prefers to develop his thought poetically and reflectively. For the sake of order and clarity here, we will recall and develop some of the major themes of his religious thought before focusing more directly on his reflections on prayer.

# I

The nature and reality of God as known and experienced by the believer was a theme that Heschel returned to over and over in his writings, since he recognized it as central to his thought. It is necessary to awaken as fully as possible to the reality of God, for in Heschel's eyes, "God is of no importance unless He is of supreme importance."[5] Before any analysis or conceptualization there must come the experience of the divine, the experience of the reality of God. First must come the experience of the reality itself and then the analysis.[6]   Thus our "knowledge" of God does not mean primarily the acquisition of new information, but the learning of a new way of seeing, a knowledge through insight.

Heschel recognized that the longing for God never subsided in the Jewish soul. Over and over the psalmist expressed this longing with such words as: "Seek ye the Lord and his strength, seek his face continually" (Ps 105:4) and "One thing have I asked of the Lord, that I will seek after, that I may abide in the house of the Lord all the days of my life, to behold the beauty of the Lord" (Ps 27:4). With this in mind, Heschel raises the practical question of how we seek God's presence, for it is on God's presence that he places great emphasis. In response he speaks about three starting points, or trails, that lead to God. The first is the way of sensing the presence of God in the world around us; the second is the way of sensing God's presence in the Bible; and the third is the way of encountering God's presence in sacred deeds. In the Jewish tradition, these three ways correspond to the three main aspects of religious existence: worship, learning and action.[7]

For our purposes here, let us focus on the first way that leads to the presence of God, the way to an awareness of God through beholding the world around us. *Lift up your eyes and see*, Heschel urges us over and over in his writings. For him, the grand premise of religion is that *"man is able to surpass himself*; that man, who is part of this world, may enter into a relationship with Him who is greater than the world; that man may lift up his mind and be attached to the absolute."[8] In developing this way to an awareness of God through beholding the world here and now, Heschel makes use of the biblical categories of the sublime, wonder, mystery, awe and glory.

Heschel sees three aspects of nature that command our

attention: its power, its loveliness and its grandeur. Power
we exploit, loveliness we enjoy and grandeur fills us with
awe. It is upon this latter aspect of grandeur that Heschel
particularly directs our attention. He will speak of this dimension in such ways as "the ineffable," "the sublime," "the
mystery" and "the holy dimension." But each signifies the
same reality, namely, "that which transcends our capacity to
understand or to express, and yet which, paradoxically, is
known to us — known by direct experience."[9]   For our
purposes here and for consistency, let us refer to this as the
dimension of the ineffable.

For Heschel, the ineffable is a dimension of all existence
and may be experienced everywhere and at all times. "We
may face it at every turn, in a grain of sand, in an atom, as
well as in stellar space. Everything holds the great secret. For
it is the inescapable situation of all being to be involved in the
infinite mystery."[10]

> The ineffable inhabits the magnificent and the
> common, the grandiose and the tiny facts of reality
> alike. Some people sense it in the ordinary events, in
> every fold, in every nook; day after day, hour after
> hour. To them things are bereft of triteness; to them
> being does not mate with nonsense. They hear the
> stillness that crowds the world in spite of our noise, in
> spite of our greed. Slight and simple as things may be
> — a piece of paper, a morsel of bread, a word, a sigh
> — they hide and guard a never-ending secret: A
> glimpse of God? Kinship with the spirit of being? An
> eternal flash of a will?[11]

Our sensitivity to the ineffable, then, must be the starting point in our search for God. Not in the sense that the
ineffable is to be equated with God. Heschel stresses the

concept of God as a presence that meets us in the dimension of the ineffable. But if we are not sensitive to this dimension, we shall hardly encounter that presence. Nor must it be thought that this sensitivity is some esoteric faculty that is limited to the few. For Heschel, it is potentially as common as sight or the ability to reason. "For just as man is endowed with the ability to know certain aspects of reality, he is endowed with the ability to know that there is more than what he knows."[12]

Yet a sensitivity to the dimension of the ineffable can easily be lost or clouded over. Radically opposed to this sensitivity and awareness would be an attitude of indifference to the wonder of living by taking things for granted or believing that "everything can be explained and that reality is a simple affair which has only to be organized in order to be mastered."[13]   For Heschel, then, maintaining the sense of awe that the ineffable gives rise to must be the chief characteristic of the religious person's attitude toward history and nature. Awe in this sense is the wonder and humility inspired by the sublime or felt in the presence of mystery. It is more than an emotion, though; it is a way of understanding, an act of insight into a meaning greater than ourselves.

For Heschel the beginning of awe is wonder and the beginning of wisdom is awe. He realistically recognizes that this is difficult to maintain, for as civilization advances, the sense of wonder declines. Even though "the whole earth is full of His glory," we do not perceive it and the perception of the glory becomes a rare occurrence as wonder is dimmed by indifference and life becomes a routine resistant to the wonder. But still for Heschel "the beginning of our happiness lies in the understanding that life without wonder is not worth living. What we lack is not a will to believe but a will to wonder."[14]   In this connection, Heschel sees as one of the goals of the Jewish way of living the experiencing of commonplace deeds as spiritual adventures. He stresses that this sense for the "continual marvels" is both the source of prayer and the spring of all creative thinking.

We might recall by way of emphasis that what is given and what we sense of the ineffable is not for Heschel the ultimate. Nature is not everything; it is only the beginning. He exhorts us:

> *Lift up your eyes on high and see who creates these.* There is a higher form of seeing. We must learn how to lift up our eyes on high in order to see that the world is more a question than an answer. The world's beauty and power are as naught compared to Him. The grandeur of nature is only the beginning. *Beyond the grandeur* is God.[15]

Thus for Heschel religion begins with wonder and mystery. Religion is the result of what a person does with the ultimate wonder, with the moments of awe, with the sense of mystery. Faith does not come into being out of nothing; "it is preceded by awe, by acts of amazement at things we apprehend but cannot comprehend."[16]  Faith is an act of persons who, transcending themselves, respond to Him who transcends the world.

As we have noted earlier, it is not only by way of the ineffable and the corresponding sense of awe that we are led to God's presence; God is present in the Bible and in sacred deeds. In fact, for Heschel, "God is more immediately found in the Bible as well as in acts of kindness and worship than in the mountains and forests."[17]  It would carry us too far afield here to develop these two ways fully, but they should be kept in mind. Heschel develops his concept of revelation and God's presence in the Bible particularly in the second part of *God in Search of Man*. We should note, though in summary form, the stress he places on the sacred deed, the *mitsvah*, as a way to God's presence. He writes:

> Indeed the concern of Judaism is primarily not how to find the presence of God in the world of things but how to let Him enter the ways in which we deal with things; how to be with Him in time, not only in space. This is why the *mitsvah* is a supreme source of religious insight and experience. . . . No one is lonely when doing a *mitsvah*, for a *mitsvah* is where God and man meet.[18]

## *II*

A second major aspect of Heschel's treatment of the mystery of God is that of the divine pathos. The influence of the Jewish prophetic tradition is strong here, as is the particular and unique interpretation of that tradition Heschel developed in his major study on the prophets.[19] He sees the divine pathos, which is basically a very active concern for all men and women on the part of God, as the central category of the prophetic understanding of God. In Heschel's view, God is not an object but a subject who reveals Himself, who cares for us, who takes a direct part in the events of the world. God does not reveal Himself in an abstract absoluteness but in a personal and intimate relation to the world.

> God does not simply command and expect obedience; He is also moved and affected by what happens in the world and reacts accordingly. Events

and human actions arouse in Him joy or sorrow, pleasure or wrath. He is not conceived as judging the world in detachment. He reacts in an intimate and subjective manner, and thus determines the value of events. Quite obviously in the biblical view, man's deeds may move Him, affect Him, grieve Him or, on the other hand, gladden and please Him. This notion that God can be intimately affected, that He possesses not merely intelligence and will, but also pathos, basically defines the prophetic consciousness of God.[20]

Pathos, then, implies loving care and an outgoing, dynamic relation between God and human beings. It is not mere feeling; but it is a free act, the result of decision and determination. The God of the prophet continues to be involved in human history and to be affected by human acts. Heschel writes:

Never in history has man been taken as seriously as in prophetic thinking. Man is not only an image of God; he is a perpetual concern of God. The idea of pathos adds a new dimension to human existence. Whatever man does affects not only his own life, but also the life of God insofar as it is directed to man. The import of man raises him beyond the level of mere creature. He is a consort, a partner, a factor in the life of God.[21]

The divine pathos has a human counterpart in Heschel's thought, and it should be noted here briefly. If God is sensed as pathos, as intimately concerned with our affairs and the world, what should be the response on our part? For Heschel, the response would be one of *sympathy*, for "when the divine is sensed as pathos, the response is one of sympathy."²² For the prophet, sympathy is the way of fulfilling in a personal manner the demand addressed to him in moments of revelation. The prophet is stirred by an intimate concern for the divine concern. That is why for Heschel being a prophet means "to identify one's concern with the concern of God."²³ Prophetic sympathy is not a momentary response but a constant attitude, a sense of challenge and commitment. It is interesting to note in passing the effect that Heschel's study on the prophets and prophetic consciousness had upon his own personal life and awareness. These studies coincide somewhat with his own emergence as a spokesman for many social issues of the day. Study of the prophets seemed to intensify his own social concern.

In connection, too, with this response of sympathy and all that it implies and involves, note should be taken of Heschel's treatment of human needs. He recognizes the importance and validity of our needs and our legitimate attempts to fulfill them. Yet he likewise stresses that we must not focus on ourselves and our deeds, making them ultimate ends in themselves. For Heschel "short is the way from need to greed." And so we must be able to rise above our needs, to transcend them in a spirit of freedom; "we must be able to say *no* to ourselves in the name of a higher *yes*."²⁴ Whereas animals are content when their own needs are satisfied, persons insist not only on being satisfied but also on being able to satisfy, on *being a need* as well as *having needs*.

Convinced that our needs are temporal while our being needed is lasting, Heschel would define happiness as the conviction and certainty of being needed. This immediately leads him to ask the question, Who is in need of man? And he answers very clearly that we are a need of God. "Man is not an innocent bystander in the cosmic drama. There is in us more kinship with the divine than we are able to believe: 'Man is needed, he is a need of God.' "[25]   Developing this idea with his concept of religion, Heschel writes:

> There is only one way to define Jewish religion. It is the *awareness of God's interest in man*, the awareness of a *covenant*, of a responsibility that lies on Him as well as on us. Our task is to concur with His interest, to carry out His vision of our task. God is in need of man for the attainment of His ends, and religion, as Jewish tradition understands it, is a way of serving these ends, of which we are in need, even though we may not be aware of them, ends which we must learn to feel the need of.[26]

# *III*

Having seen these general aspects of Heschel's religious thought, we are in a better position to focus on his reflections on prayer itself. As noted before, Heschel does not present us with any systematic treatment of prayer. He tends to write around the subject, coming at it in a somewhat repetitive way and from different perspectives. It should be kept in mind also that he does not write on prayer in any detached and analytical way. His approach is that of a person profoundly convinced of the value, importance and centrality of prayer in his own life and the religious lives of all believers. His intense, poetic and moving style reflects this concern.

In speaking of prayer Heschel makes use of the classical statement of rabbinic literature "Know before whom you stand" to summarize many of his reflections, since it answers the question, "What is it that a person is conscious of in moments of prayer?" For the sake of clarity, we will consider this statement in some detail. The phrases "know," "before whom" and "you stand" are all-important for him.

Heschel uses the word "know" in the sense of *insight*, realizing that a certain understanding or awareness is a necessity. He recognizes that emotion is an important component of prayer but must take second place to insight. He writes:

> The true source of prayer is not an emotion but an insight. It is the insight into the mystery of reality, *the sense of the ineffable*, that enables us to pray. As long as we refuse to take notice of what is beyond our sight, beyond our reason; as long as we are blind to the mystery of being, the way to prayer is closed to us.[27]

But not only is insight a prerequisite of all prayer, prayer itself has the power to generate insight, endowing us with an understanding that speculation cannot attain. Often when reflection fails, prayer succeeds; for prayer can go beyond speculation. In this sense prayer is a way to faith, and some of our deepest spiritual insights are born in moments of prayer. Heschel recognized, too, that such insight and understanding do not come automatically and easily. The art of the awareness of God, the art of sensing His presence in our daily lives cannot be learned offhand.

Recalling the continual emphasis Heschel places upon acts of wonder and radical amazement as the ways to prayer, we might note that prayer itself keeps alive the sense of wonder in our lives. As Heschel writes: "To pray is to take notice of the wonder, to regain a sense of the mystery that animates all beings, the divine margin in all attainments.

Prayer is our humble answer to the inconceivable surprise of living. It is all we can offer in return for the mystery by which we live."[28]

In referring to the phrase "before whom" in the classical statement quoted above, Heschel returns to the familiar theme of the reality of God. More than once Heschel stresses that "*the issue of prayer is not prayer; the issue of prayer is God.* One cannot pray unless he has faith in his own ability to accost the infinite, merciful, eternal God."[29]  It is important that God be real to us, that we be convinced of God's reality and our ability to transcend ourselves and accost the ultimate. For Heschel, "unless God is at least as real as my own self, unless I am sure that God has at least as much life as I do, how could I pray? If God does not have the power to speak to us, how should we possess the power to speak to Him? If God is unable to listen to men, then I am insane in talking to Him."[30]

For Heschel, then, as he is so fond of saying, "God is of no importance unless He is of supreme importance." In this regard, he stresses that it is important for us to realize that we have the power to surpass ourselves. We must realize that the self is more than the self and that our highest concern is not our own concern. In other words, we have the capacity to attach ourselves to the utmost, and it is through prayer that we do so. In fact, to be fully ourselves, to be fully human, we must transcend ourselves. Heschel writes:

> Prayer is our attachment to the utmost. Without
> God in sight we are like the scattered rungs of a
> broken ladder. To pray is to become a ladder
> on which thoughts mount to God to join the move-
> ment toward Him which surges unnoticed through-
> out the entire universe. We do not step out of the
> world when we pray; we merely see the world in

a different setting. The self is not the hub, but the spoke of the revolving wheel. In prayer we shift the center of living from self-consciousness to self-surrender. God is the center toward which all forces tend. He is the source, and we are the flowing of His force, the ebb and flow of His tides.[31]

Thus for Heschel the basis of prayer is the conviction of our ability to accost God and to lay our hopes, sorrows and wishes before Him. We can approach and draw near to God because God has first approached and drawn near to us. "Before the words of prayer come to the lips, the mind must believe in God's willingness to draw near to us, and in our ability to clear the path for His approach."[32]

It might appear that the capacity to attach ourselves to the utmost through prayer is something extra or merely desirable. Heschel is insistent that this is not the case, stressing that to be fully ourselves we must go beyond ourselves. He writes: "As a tree torn from the soil, as a river separated from its source, the human soul wanes when detached from what is greater than itself. . . . Unless we aspire to the utmost, we shrink to inferiority."[33]   In other words, Heschel regards prayer as an ontological necessity on our part, and in this sense the problem is not how to revitalize prayer but how to revitalize ourselves. Speaking of this necessity, he writes: "Prayer is not a need but *an ontological necessity*; an act that constitutes the very essence of man. He who has never prayed is not fully human. Ontology, not psychology or sociology, explains prayer."[34]

The phrase "you stand" in our statement "Know before whom you stand" focuses more directly on our relationship with God. It looks more at our attitude, our orientation, our decision to enter and face the presence of God. "To pray means to expose oneself to Him, to His judgment." When we pray we become open to the Presence we could evade, the Presence that will not intrude itself upon us. As Heschel puts it: "Prayer is an invitation to God to intervene in our lives, to let His will prevail in our affairs; it is the opening of a window to Him in our will, an effort to make Him the Lord of our soul. We submit our interests to His concern, and seek to be allied with what is ultimately right." Thus through prayer we bring God back into the world to establish His kingship. "Great is the power of prayer," Heschel writes. "For to worship is *to expand the presence of God* in the world. God is transcendent, but our worship makes Him immanent."[35]

# *IV*

In the context of his treatment of Jewish prayer, Heschel is particularly concerned about one specific difficulty that is common to all systems and forms of prayer and is certainly applicable to Christian prayer. There are laws on when to pray, how to pray and what to pray. There are fixed times, fixed ways and fixed texts. On the other hand, prayer has to be worship of the heart, the outpouring of the soul, a matter of *kavanah*, that is, of *inner devotion.* Heschel puts it this way: "Jewish prayer is uniformity and individuality, law and freedom, a duty and a prerogative, empathy and self-expression, insight and sensitivity, creed and faith, the word and that which is beyond words."[36]

Heschel looks upon these as the two principles about which Jewish prayer revolves. He sees, however, that each of the two poles moves in the opposite direction; as a result, equilibrium can be maintained only if both are of equal force. He realistically admits that "the pole of regularity usually proves to be stronger than the pole of spontaneity and as a result, there is perpetual danger of prayer becoming a mere habit, a mechanical performance, an exercise in repetitiousness. The fixed pattern and regularity of our services tends to stifle the spontaneity of devotion."[37]   For Heschel, then, the great problem in the polarity is not to let the principle of regularity impair the power of spontaneity.

Given this observation and conviction, Heschel goes on to make some interesting and helpful remarks regarding this basic tension in prayer. His observations are very applicable to Christian and other forms of prayer, since all praying persons are involved with the same basic tension.

Although seeing the necessity, then, of maintaining an equilibrium between what he refers to as inwardness (*agada*) and law (*halacha*), Heschel does not hesitate to give greater importance to inwardness. For him, "prayer becomes trivial when ceasing to be an act in the soul. The essence of prayer is *agada*, inwardness."[38]   He stresses this because he realizes that often prayer becomes a mere lip service or obligation to be discharged. Heschel is convinced that prayer must have life. It must not become a drudgery, with one just going through the motions; it must not be just a ceremony, an act of mere respect for tradition. For this reason, Heschel stresses that "the problem is not how to revitalize prayer; the problem is how to revitalize ourselves."[39]

The spirit Heschel is referring to when he speaks of revitalizing ourselves and creating a new heart is the spirit of *kavanah*. He doesn't give a set definition of the word, for it seems to elude a simple description. We find him referring to it in such terms as: "Prayer without *kavanah* is like a body without a soul." "*Kavanah* is more than attentiveness, more than the state of being aware of what we are saying. . . . It is attentiveness to God, an act of appreciation of being able to stand in the presence of God."[40]   Thus *kavanah* is insight, appreciation, awareness. For Heschel, it is simply a matter of *kavanah* being indispensable to prayer:

> To pray is to pull ourselves together, to pour our
> perception, volition, memory, thought, hope, feel-
> ing, dreams, all that is moving in us, into one tone.
> Not the words we utter, the service of the lips, but
> the way in which the devotion of the heart cor-
> responds to what the words contain, the conscious-
> ness of speaking under His eyes, is the pith of
> prayer.[41]

*Kavanah* is something that requires constant effort and we
may meet more failure than success. But for Heschel the
struggle for *kavanah* must continue if we are not to die of
spiritual paralysis.

In an address to fellow rabbis, Heschel stresses the rabbi's role in bringing about a spirit of *kavanah*. He pleads
strongly for a prayer atmosphere that is created not by
ceremonies, gimmicks, or speeches, but by the example of a
person who prays:

> The rabbi's role in the sacred hour of worship goes
> far beyond that of maintaining order and decorum.
> His unique task is to be a source of inspiration, to
> endow others with a sense of *kavanah*. And as we
> have said, *kavanah* is more than a touch of
> emotion. *Kavanah* is insight, appreciation. To
> acquire such insight, to deepen such appreciation is
> something *we must learn* all the days of our lives. Such
> insight, such appreciation, we must convey to others.
> It may be difficult to convey to others what we think,
> but it is not difficult to convey to others *what we live*.
> Our task is to echo and to reflect the light and spirit
> of prayer.[42]

Reflecting the familiar principle that one cannot give what one does not possess, Heschel stresses the role of prayer in the life of the rabbi. If the main purpose of being a rabbi is to bring persons closer to the Father in heaven, then one of his supreme tasks is to pray and to teach others how to pray. Heschel writes:

> To be able to inspire people to pray one must love his people, understand their predicaments and be sensitive to the power of exaltation, purification and sanctification hidden in our prayer book. To attain sensitivity he must commune with the great masters of the past, and learn how to pour his own dreams and anxieties into the well of prayer.[43]

Finally, in speaking about preaching to his fellow rabbis, Heschel links the sermon directly to prayer. For him, preaching is not an end in itself; it is either an organic part of the art of prayer or it is out of place. He urges his fellow rabbis: "Preach in order to pray. The test of a true sermon is that it can be converted to prayer."[44]

Having established the primacy of inwardness (*agada*) and the importance of *kavanah*, Heschel would not have us forget the other pole, namely that of *halacha*, the need for law, structure, observance. In his mind the aim is equilibrium and balance:

> The essence of prayer is *agada*, inwardness. Yet it would be a tragic failure not to appreciate what the spirit of *halacha* does for it, raising it from the level of an individual act to that of an eternal intercourse between the people Israel and God; from the level of an occasional experience to that of a permanent

covenant. It is through *halacha* that we belong to God
not occasionally, intermittently, but essentially,
continually. Regularity of prayer is an expression of
my belonging to an order, to the covenant between
God and Israel, which remains valid regardless of
whether I am conscious of it or not.[45]

In his essay "Continuity Is the Way" Heschel has some
interesting reflections on discipline and observance. He is in
strong disagreement with those who are horrified by the
suggestion of accepting a daily discipline. In his mind they
are really unfree and are confusing inner control with external tyranny. The goal and the way cannot long endure in
separation. "Unless the outer life expresses the inner world,
piety stagnates and intention decays."[46]   Since the goal is
great, the way must be directed.

All of this naturally leads Heschel to a study of the law
and to an analysis of the meaning of observance. He recognizes that we are not always in the mood to pray and that
we do not always have the vision and the strength to say a
word in the presence of God. It is here that the law comes to
our rescue, for "when I am weak, it is the law that gives me
strength; when my vision is dim, it is duty that gives me
insight."[47]   A great source of consolation for Heschel is the
realization and conviction that there is something far
greater than my desire to pray, namely, God's desire that I
pray, just as there is something far greater than my will to
believe, namely, God's will that I believe.

Heschel attributes great importance to maintaining the
sense of the whole and sustaining a strong sense of belonging to the spiritual order of Jewish living. For him the Jewish
form of living lies not so much with the performance of
single good deeds as "the state of being committed to the
task of belonging to an order in which single deeds,

aggregates of religious feeling, sporadic sentiments, moral episodes become parts of a complete pattern."[48]   To maintain the sense of the *whole*, one must take religious observance seriously.

Heschel is convinced, too, that there must be no separation between prayer and the rest of life. Prayer is certainly at the essence of the spiritual life, but one cannot rest content with essences. Thus it is necessary "to care for the meaning that is found in deeds, to sense the holy that is available in the everyday, to be devoted to the daily as much as the extraordinary, to be concerned for the cycle as much as for the special event."[49]   For Heschel, it is not a question of having faith in deeds but of attaining faith through deeds. He is fond of stressing how important it is for a person to take a leap of action and "to do more than he understands in order to understand more than he does." Thus the deed is the source of holiness for Heschel. In fact, Judaism stands and falls with the idea of the absolute relevance of human deeds, for "faith is but a seed, while the deed is its growth or decay."[50]

One final point may be noted here: Heschel's emphasis on our being the symbol of God; we are created in the image and likeness of God. Heschel spells out some far-reaching implications of this. First, reverence for God is shown in our reverence for all other persons. "Our fear of offending or hurting a human being must be as ultimate as our fear of God. An act of violence is an act of desecration. To be arrogant toward man is to be blasphemous toward God."[51]   Second, what is necessary for us is not to *have* a symbol but to *be* a symbol. The divine symbolism for us is not, according to Heschel, in what we have but in what we are potentially: to be holy as God is holy. We can enhance our likeness to God by imitating Him and by acting as God acts in mercy and love.

\*    \*    \*    \*    \*    \*    \*

Such, then, is Abraham Heschel's legacy of prayer, rich in the witness of the man's own life and in the moving thoughts of his writings. We might close with a passage that is characteristic of the prophetic intensity of his message in its clear impatience of half measures and insistence upon the fullest response to God:

> God will return to us when we shall be willing to let Him into our banks and factories, into our Congress and clubs, into our courts and investigating committees, into our homes and theaters. For God is everywhere or nowhere, the Father of all men or no man, concerned about everything or nothing. Only in His presence shall we learn that the glory of man is not in his will to power, but in his power of compassion. Man reflects either the image of His presence or that of a beast.[52]

---

1  One of the most knowledgeable interpreters of Heschel's thought writes: "Abraham Joshua Heschel is the product of two different worlds. His life and work can perhaps best be understood as an attempt to achieve a creative viable synthesis between the traditional piety and learning of Eastern European Jewry and the philosophy and scholarship of Western civilization." Fritz A. Rothschild, ed., *Between God and Man* (New York: The Free Press, 1965), p. 7.

2  John C. Bennett writes: "Abraham Heschel belonged to the whole religious community. I know of no other person of whom this was so true. . . . Christians are nourished in their own faith by his vision and his words." See the special Heschel edition of *America* (March 10, 1973), p. 205. The entire issue of this periodical was devoted to Heschel and published shortly after his death.

3  *Ibid.*, p. 202.

4  *The Documents of Vatican II*, ed. Walter M. Abbott (New York: America Press, 1966), p. 665.

5  Heschel, *Man's Quest for God* (New York: Scribner's, 1954), p. xiii.

6  For Heschel, the task of the philosophy of religion is the analysis of "concrete events, acts, insights, of that which is immediately given with the pious man." *Man Is Not Alone* (New York: Harper Torchbooks, 1966), p. 55.

7  Heschel, *God in Search of Man* (New York: Harper Torchbooks, 1966), p. 31. The three main sections of this book correspond to these three ways.

8  *Ibid.*, p. 33.

9  Franklin Sherman, *The Promise of Heschel* (Philadelphia: Lippincott, 1970), p. 25.

10  *God in Search of Man*, p. 57.

11  *Man Is Not Alone*, p. 5. It is interesting to note how similar this passage is to a passage from the Trappist monk Thomas Merton: "Every moment and every event of every man's life on earth plants something in his soul." *New Seeds of Contemplation* (New York: New Directions, 1961), p. 14.

12  *Man Is Not Alone*, p. 20.

13  *God in Search of Man*, p. 43.

14  *Ibid.*, p. 46. Heschel also writes: "There is no worship, no love, if we take for granted the blessings or defeats of living." *Ibid.*, p. 49.

15  *Ibid.*, p. 97.

16  *Ibid.*, p. 153.

17  *Ibid.*, pp. 311-312.

18  *Ibid.*, p. 312.

19  Heschel, *The Prophets* (2 vols; New York: Harper Torchbooks, 1971). Heschel writes: "There are two poles of prophetic thinking: the idea that God is one, holy, different and apart from all that exists, and the idea of the inexhaustible concern of God for man, at times brightened by His mercy, at times darkened by His anger. He is both transcendent, beyond human understanding and full of love, compassion, grief or anger." *Man Is Not Alone*, p. 224.

20  *The Prophets*, II, p. 4.

21  *Ibid.*, p. 6.

22  *Ibid.*, p. 89.

23  *Ibid.*

24  *Man Is Not Alone*, pp. 188, 189.

25  *Ibid.*, p. 215. Heschel also writes: "Judaism shows it to be a need *to be needed by God*. It teaches us that every man is in need of God because God is in need of men. Our need of Him is but an echo of His need of us." *Ibid.*, p. 248.

26  *Ibid.*, p. 241.

27  *Man's Quest for God*, pp. 62-63.

28  *Ibid.*, p. 5.

29  *Ibid.*, p. 58. See also p. 87.

30  *Ibid.*, p. 89. See also p. 97. In general Heschel is reluctant to speak of prayer as dialogue. He feels a better metaphor would be to describe prayer as an act of immersion. See his essay "Prayer as Discipline" in *The Insecurity of Freedom* (New York: Farrar, Straus, and Giroux, 1965), p. 255.

31  *Man's Quest for God*, p. 7.

32  *Ibid.*, pp. 9-10. Heschel also writes: "Prayer is the approach of the human to the transcendent. Prayer makes man a relative to the sublime, initiating him into the mystery." *Ibid.*, p. 13.

33  *Ibid.*, pp. 6-7.

34  *Ibid.*, p. 78.

35  *Ibid.*, pp. 61, 15-16, 62.

36  *Ibid.*, pp. 64-65.

37  *Ibid.*, p. 65.

38  *Ibid.*, p. 68.

39  *Ibid.*, p. 77. In a similar vein, while referring to the prayer book, Heschel notes: "What we need is a revision of the soul, a new heart rather than a new text." *Ibid.*, p. 83.

40  *Ibid.*, p. 84.

41  *Ibid.*, p. 13.

42  *Ibid.*, pp. 85-86.

43  *Ibid.*, p. 76.

44  *Ibid.*, p. 80.

45  *Ibid.*, p. 68.

46  *Ibid.*, p. 93.

47  *Ibid.*, p. 97.

48  *Man Is Not Alone*, p. 270.

49  *Man's Quest for God*, p. 94. We might note in passing here the similarity in thought with St. Ignatius Loyola's concepts in his *Spiritual Exercises* of finding God in all things and being "contemplatives in action."

50  *Ibid.*, pp. 106, 110.

51  *Ibid.*, p. 125.

52  *Ibid.*, pp. 150-151.

# Thomas
# MERTON (1915-1968)

PRAYER OCCUPIED a central position in the life and writings of the well-known Trappist monk and writer, Thomas Merton. The practice of prayer was at the heart of his monastic vocation and in his voluminous writings the subject of prayer was a constant and overriding interest. In fact, as one looks at the corpus of Merton's writings and the primary position prayer played in his own life, one faces the challenge of selecting from a vast area. Hopefully, this essay will capture some of the essence and flavor of his legacy of prayer.

It would seem best to look at Merton's own life and his own prayerful experience of God. This would suggest itself for a number of reasons. First, Merton has provided us with an abundance of personal data through his autobiographical works and various journals. Secondly, much of Merton's spiritual writings flowed from his own experience of God, from his own lived experience as a monk and a man of prayer. It is clear from *The Seven Storey Mountain* and his other autobiographical works that Merton was touched deeply by God's grace. He in turn sought to respond fully and give himself completely to God in the seeking and fulfilling of His will. The phrase "God alone" always moved him deeply.

Throughout his life, Merton remained a searcher. He sought the truth about himself and about his own existence with relentless sincerity and intensity. Although he certainly found God in his life, he continued to search for a deeper union with his Creator. It is interesting to note that *The Seven Storey Mountain* closes with the Latin phrase, "Sit finis libri, non finis quaerendi" ("Let it be the end of the book, but not the end of the searching"). With this in mind let us look at Merton's own search for God and his own spiritual odyssey before focusing on his writings on prayer.

# I

Religion and prayer played very little part in Merton's early years. He received no religious upbringing or education during these years and so religion and the concept of God remained only mysterious terms for him. Although there were some contacts with the practice of religion (such as the time he and his father stayed with the Private family in France) and with institutional religion (during his years in various boarding schools), none of these early experiences touched him very significantly.

His first real religious experience came during his stay in Rome when he was making a tour of Europe just before he began his studies at Cambridge University. A fascination with the Byzantine mosaics in the old Roman churches he visited led to a religious awakening and a desire to learn more about the Christ who was portrayed so vividly in them. It led him to the pages of the New Testament with the desire "to find out something of Who this Person was that men called Christ."[1]   This led in turn to a temporary religious conversion which he describes vividly in his autobiography. He was alone at night in his room and suddenly he sensed the presence of his father who had been dead more than a year. The sense of that presence passed in a flash but he was left with a profound insight into his own condition at the time. Overwhelmed and disgusted by what he saw, he instinctively prayed for some release.

> And now I think for the first time in my whole life I really began to pray — praying not with my lips and with my intellect and my imagination, but praying out of the very roots of my life and of my being, and praying to the God I had never known, to reach down towards me out of His darkness and to help me to get free of the thousand terrible things that held my will in their slavery.[2]

This experience left him with a strong desire to change the course of his life. He continued to pray and to read the New Testament, but it was not to last at this time. In a matter of some months this real but temporary religious fervor cooled and eventually disappeared. In fact, the following year, his first and only year at Cambridge University, turned out to be one of the unhappiest years of his life and led directly to his permanent move to the United States to live with his grandparents.

Merton's earnest seeking of God would begin during his early years as a student at Columbia University in the middle 1930s. Although it would take him through many winding roads, it would never be interrupted again.

Various books and persons proved to be instrumental in leading him to God and to a deep and pervasive religious faith. For example, he tells us in *The Seven Storey Mountain* of the impact Etienne Gilson's book, *The Spirit of Medieval Philosophy*, had upon him once he overcame his repugnance upon learning it was a Catholic book. He was struck by the

Latin term "aseitas" and the concept of God as pure being and uncaused cause that this scholastic term conveyed to him so powerfully. Merton spoke of this realization as a special grace of God and something that was to revolutionize his whole life.[3]   He also highlighted the influence of Aldous Huxley's book, *Ends and Means*, for it was here that he became acquainted with the writings of St. John of the Cross, St. Teresa of Avila and other Christian mystics and spiritual writers.

Merton would look back, too, and recognize clearly and appreciatively the significant role human friendship played under God's providence in leading him to the light of faith and a religious commitment during his student years at Columbia. Mark Van Doren, a gifted teacher and friend; Bob Lax, a classmate and special friend in many ways; Dan Walsh, teacher of Thomism and a support and guide to Merton in his religious vocation; Bramachari, a Hindu monk — these and others influenced him positively and powerfully. All of these instruments of God's grace and his own searching, praying and reflecting finally led to his baptism in the Catholic Church in 1938.

Three more years would elapse before Merton would become a Cistercian monk of the strict observance. These three years were a time of spiritual growth and the further seeking of God's will for the young convert, as he continued studying, writing and teaching at Columbia and later St. Bonaventure's College. Although he later regretted the absence of some spiritual direction at this important time of his life, he prayerfully sought the Lord through the sacraments, the reading of the Breviary, retreats, spiritual reading, etc. The path he followed continued to be a somewhat winding one, but it seemed to lead inexorably to his entrance into the Cistercian (Trappist) Abbey of Our Lady of Gethsemani in December of 1941.

Merton's entrance into the monastery was the end of one stage in his life and the beginning of another. He was in his 27th year at the time, and he would remain a faithful member of that monastery until his sudden death 27 years later. His early years as a monk continued to be a time of growth, of searching, and of the resolution of some vocational difficulties.

Gethsemani Abbey provided Merton with a firm basis of acceptance, warmth and security that brought about the peace and interior freedom he needed to grow as a person and a monk. With this growth, there gradually developed in his life a sense of wholeness, of unity and of purpose. This came only with time, patient discipline, persevering effort and continual generosity to God's working in his life.

First of all, Gethsemani provided Merton with a place where he could sink roots deeply. This was the first time that he really was able to do this given the history of constant change in his life, and it proved to be enormously significant for his personal growth. He became part of a community that was supportive and one to which he felt a deep sense of "belonging." Secondly, Gethsemani provided Merton with the opportunity to receive regular and capable spiritual direction. This proved invaluable in two important areas: discerning the attraction Merton felt for the Carthusian way of life with its greater solitude; and resolving the difficulties he initially had reconciling his vocation as a monk and his work as a writer.[4]   Finally, Gethsemani provided Merton with the atmosphere he needed to experience God's love and forgiveness at a profound level through the silence, the solitude and the prayerful atmosphere which it provided. Here God's grace worked with its healing prower:

> It was true. I was hidden in the secrecy of His protection. He was surrounding me constantly with the

work of His love, His wisdom and His mercy. And so
it would be, day after day, year after year. Sometimes
I would be preoccupied with problems that seemed
to be difficult and seemed to be great, and yet when
it was all over the answers that I worked out did not
seem to matter much anyway, because all the while,
beyond my range of vision and comprehension, God
had silently and perceptibly worked the whole thing
out for me, and had presented me with the solution.
To say it better, He had worked the solution into the
very tissue of my own life and substance and existence by the wise incomprehensible weaving of His
Providence.[5]

If Merton's early years at Gethsemani were marked by
an inward thrust as he sought to grow as a person and a
monk, and also to resolve some of the identity questions that
still remained for him, the years beginning with the early
1950s were marked by a decidedly outward thrust. Having
experienced the love and compassion of God in his own life,
he grew in his own spirit of love and compassion towards
others. This outward thrust manifested itself in the work he
assumed in the monastery after completing his own
monastic and priestly training. He was asked to share the
fruits of his own prayer and reflective study through the
teaching and directing of others within his own community.
From 1951 until 1955, he was the Master of Scholastics; and
from 1955 until 1965, he was directly involved in the
monastic formation of others in the important position of
Master of Novices. He himself was pleasantly surprised that
these responsibilities not only did not take him away from a
spirit of prayer and silence, but gave it a new depth and
dimension.[6]

There was certainly, too, an outward thrust to his writings. This manifested itself particularly in the breadth and scope of his subject matter. Much of his published works in the 1950s and 60s dealt with the important social and political issues and problems of the day. Merton himself saw this increased social awareness as the natural outgrowth of his prayer and solitude. His constant interest in contemplation and mystical thought also led him to explore the riches of Eastern thought and spirituality in the 1960s. In fact, his untimely death in 1968 came in Bangkok, Thailand, during the course of an Eastern journey. This was his first extended trip away from the monastery, and he had long awaited the opportunity to study and observe at firsthand some of the Eastern spiritual traditions.

## *II*

It should be helpful here to look a little more closely at some aspects of Merton's life and activity. First of all, his vocation as a monk was at the center of his life and he always strived to give himself to that call faithfully and generously. The inscription above the door at Gethsemani, "God Alone," always spoke to him deeply. Questions might arise over the course of his monastic life as to what particular form it should take, but there was no doubt in his mind of his vocation as a monk. There was a basic conviction and commitment regarding his monastic vocation that took precedence over everything else. One will never understand Merton and his life unless this is realized. First and foremost Thomas Merton was a monk and he was ever grateful to God for his monastic vocation.[7]   Over the years, as he grew and matured in his own life as a monk, his understanding and appreciation of monasticism grew and clarified. His abundant and insightful writings on the monastic life attest to this.

Writing was always a major part of Merton's life. His first published work, a book of poetry, came out shortly after his entrance into Gethsemani, but he was continuously occupied with various writing projects throughout the years before he became a Trappist monk.[8]   This would continue throughout his years at Gethsemani, and his output in this area would be enormous. However, the primacy he wanted to give to his monastic vocation in large part was the reason for the difficulty Merton initially experienced in reconciling his successful and absorbing writing with his vocation as a monk. This caused much tension and conflict, particularly after the widespread success of *The Seven Storey Mountain* following its publication in 1948. Merton gives us a glimpse of this struggle to integrate the monk and the writer in the epilogue to *The Seven Storey Mountain* (where he writes of "this shadow, this double, this writer who had followed me into the cloister")[9] and in many of his entries in *The Sign of Jonas.*

The steady encouragement of his superiors and the reassurance he received from them that his writing was compatible with his Trappist vocation and with his desire for a deep union with God helped a great deal in bringing about the necessary reconciliation in Merton's mind. He came to see that he could love and serve God through his writings and that these could be a source of spiritual good for others. His Trappist superiors obviously recognized not only his great talents as a writer and the great good he could accomplish through his writings, but also what writing meant to Merton as a person and the role it had to play in his life.[10]   Merton hints at what this steady encouragement and reassurance meant to him in a poignant passage about his first abbot, Dom Frederic Dunn. Referring to the publication of *The Seven Storey Mountain*, Merton writes:

> I shall never forget the simplicity and affection with which he put the first copy of the book in my hand. He did not say anything. He just handed me the book, amused at my surprise. But I knew that he was happier about it than I could ever be. A few days later, he was telling me to go on writing, to love God, to be a man of prayer and humility, a monk and a contemplative, and to help other men penetrate the mystery of the love of God. It was the last time I ever spoke to him or saw him alive, because that night he died.[11]

Although writing occupied much of Merton's time and attention, for many years it took second place to his activity as a spiritual director. Outside of the monastery, Merton was known to a large segment of the public as a monk-writer, but in the monastic family at Gethsemani he was known more as a spiritual director. Shortly after his own final profession as a Trappist and his ordination to the priesthood, he was asked to assume responsibilities as a spiritual director towards those younger in the religious life. This work was to increase, particularly during his ten years as Master of Novices, abating only when he retired to his hermitage in 1965. He doesn't say a great deal about his direction of others but from some of his brief allusions, it is clear that he did it well and that he enjoyed doing it. He evidently realized how important and how privileged it was to assist others to meet God in prayer and grow in His love. In his early journal he writes of how the direction of the scholastics at Gethsemani and his contact with them helped him personally, particularly in his own prayer and in his desire for solitude.

It is from his fellow monks that we would expect to find the best witness to his capacity and ability as a spiritual director, especially those who experienced his direction personally. His abbot of many years, James Fox, who had Merton as his regular confessor for fifteen years, speaks of Merton "as a gifted director of others in the spiritual life."[12]   Flavian Burns, the abbot of Gethsemani at the time of Merton's death, delivered the homily at a Memorial Mass for Merton in which he tells us more of this aspect of Merton's life and work. Speaking of one who was "the best of spiritual fathers," Abbot Burns says:

> Still, he had a secret prayer and this is what gave the inner life to all he said and wrote. His secret was his secret to himself to a great extent, but he was a skillful reader to the secret of the souls that sought his help. It was because of this that although we laughed at him, and with him, as we would a younger Brother, still we respected him as the spiritual father of our souls.
>
> Those of us who had the privilege and pleasure to deal with Father Louis on intimate terms, and submit our inner lives to his direction, know that in him we had the best of Spiritual Fathers.[13]

As a spiritual director for his fellow monks, Merton would be continually involved in their efforts to find God in prayer and to grow in a spirit of prayer. Obviously Merton was sensitive and responsive to God's grace working deep within those who sought a life of continuous prayer as monks. It is interesting to note that although Merton directed others with great skill and wrote with great eloquence on the spiritual life, he manifested a certain reluctance to write much about his own prayer before God. Although he plunged himself into prayer, there seemed to be, as Abbot Burns indicates, areas of his prayer that remained a secret to himself and the God he sought so intensely.

This seems to be connected with Merton's strong desire to lose himself in God alone and give himself completely to a life of solitude and contemplation. Merton had a strong attraction and a strong personal need for much solitude. He recognized that the measure and degree of solitude would vary from person to person, but of himself he would write: "I am not defending a phony 'hermit-mystique,' but some of us *have to be* alone to be ourselves. Call it privacy if you like. But we have thinking to do and work to do which demands a certain silence and aloneness. We need time to do our job of meditation and creation."[14]

The life of a hermit was always close to Thomas Merton's heart. In the fall of 1965, after completing ten years as Master of Novices, Merton received permission from his superiors to live as a hermit in a small hermitage in the woods not far from the abbey. For the final three years of his life at Gethsemani, he lived as a hermit. At this time it involved a novel and pioneering move, since the Trappists are basically a community-oriented monastic group. But it was a move well suited to Merton's maturity as a monk and his search for deeper silence and solitude and more perfect contemplation.[15]

## *III*

Let us turn now from the person himself to his thought and writings. In Merton's case both seem so closely intertwined that it is difficult to separate his thought from his life. Merton *lived* his belief and in many ways his life was his message. The more we understand Merton the man, the better we can understand his writings, particularly his re-flections on prayer.

Although Merton's writings ranged far and wide in their scope and interest, he himself always sensed a unifying strand. Upon the opening of the Thomas Merton Collection in the Bellarmine College library in Louisville on November 10, 1963, Merton prepared a statement for the occasion. He wrote at this time:

> Whatever I may have written, I think it all can
> be reduced in the end to this one root truth: that God
> calls human persons to union with Himself and with
> one another in Christ, in the Church which is His
> Mystical Body. It is also a witness to the fact that
> there is and must be, in the Church, a contemplative
> life which has no other function than to realize
> these mysterious things, and to return to God all
> the thanks and praise that human hearts can give
> Him. . . . But if I have written about interracial
> justice, or thermonuclear weapons, it is because
> these issues are terribly relevant to one great truth:
> that man is called to live as a son of God. Man must
> respond to this call to live in peace with all his
> brothers in the One Christ.[16]

Abbot Flavian Burns also captures the unity of Merton's thought in the homily he delivered after Merton's death:

> Each of you, I am sure, would read his message
> somewhat differently and this, of course, is the way
> he would have it. But the message is basically the
> same for all. We are men of God only insofar as we
> are seeking God, and God will only be found by us

insofar as we find Him in truth about ourselves. The
end of all is purity of faith and love, and the thing
that keeps us going is our hope.[17]

Mention should be made, too, of Merton's basic stance
and orientation in his writing. He did not want to be known
as an "inspirational writer" nor as some authority in the area
of the spiritual life. Any notion of the "professional holy
man" or "guru" was anathema to him. He looked upon
himself more as a guide who sought to share his own experiences of God with his readers and hopefully assist them to
find God a little more in their own lives — "to help other
men penetrate the mystery of the love of God." Merton was
and is an excellent guide in our own search for God. He
speaks of this aspect in the introduction to *New Seeds of
Contemplation*:

> For this is the kind of book that achieves an effect
> that is not and cannot be controlled by any human
> author. If you can bring yourself, somehow, to read
> it in communion with the God in Whose Presence it
> was written, it will interest you and you will probably
> draw some fruit from it, more by His grace than by
> the author's efforts.[18]

## Prayer

Merton always stressed that prayer should be as simple
and natural as breathing. Prayer should be our life; it should
come from the ground of our life. We should avoid making
an issue of prayer or letting it become a cause or a project.
Merton sees that when we make a cause or an issue out of
something, we begin to oppose it to something else: "This is

prayer, this isn't. This is something sacred, this isn't." The focus could then shift to the issue rather than the reality, and prayer could then be viewed as something complicated and artificial. According to Merton, prayer should be the activity in which we are most ourselves. If prayer becomes a project for us, we can begin to play a role; it can then take on artificial elements.

For Merton, prayer is a question of a vocation, not a role. It involves us in a response to a personal call. It is God who calls us to prayer, so prayer is simply a response to God's call. God calls us to the particular form of prayer He wants from us, so we may pray in different ways. For example, He may call some to the praying of the Psalms; others to a loving attention to Him; others to the meditation of His Word in the Scriptures, etc. Although the form of prayer may vary, all prayer is basically a response to the invitation and call of a loving God.[19]

There is also a down to earth and practical thrust to Merton's approach to prayer. With his strong attraction to getting at the heart of things born of his own prayer in solitude, he manifested a reluctance to talk too much about prayer. For him, talking was not the principal thing. He insisted that "nothing that anyone says will be that important. The great thing is prayer. Prayer itself. If you want a life of prayer the way to get to it is by praying."[20]

It has been frequently noted that the idea of "connections" was filled with a mysterious significance for Thomas Merton. To start where you are and to become aware of the connections — that was his approach to prayer.[21] For Merton, building a life of prayer was not done through horizontal progress as in so many other areas of life:

In prayer we discover what we already have. You start where you are, you deepen what you already have, and you realize that you are already there. We already have everything, but we don't know it and we don't experience it. Everything has been given to us in Christ. All we need is to experience what we already possess.[22]

This does not come about automatically and so it is necessary to give time to prayer. Merton urges us:

If we really want prayer, we'll have to give it time. We must slow down to a human tempo and we'll begin to have time to listen. And as soon as we listen to what's going on, things will begin to take shape by themselves. . . . the whole thing boils down to giving ourselves in prayer a chance to realize that we have what we seek. We don't have to rush after it. It is there all the time, and if we give it time it will make itself known to us.[23]

Thus Merton has a very contemplative approach to time and its necessity for experiencing what we already possess. He recognizes the unfolding of mystery in time and he had a profound reverence for gradual growth. In his mind we should let this growing unfold in our prayer.

As would be expected from one whose monastic vocation was at the center of his spiritual life, Merton constantly affirms the primacy of contemplation, the prayer of mystical union with God. Although he never tires of stressing the importance and loftiness of contemplation, he frequently treats various other forms of prayer and meditation that prepare and dispose the person for contemplation. As Merton pointed out in his early book, *Seeds of Contemplation*: "We ordinarily have to labor to prepare ourselves in our own way and with the help of his grace, by deepening our knowledge and love of God in meditation and active forms of prayer, as well as by setting our wills free from attachments to created things."[24]   Thus in his writings we frequently find him offering suggestions about such forms of prayer as mental prayer, silent prayer, continual prayer, the prayerful reading known as "lectio divina," etc.[25]

Among these different forms of prayer that prepare for contemplation, Merton devotes a certain amount of attention to the traditional form known as mental prayer or meditation. The unitive and loving knowledge that reaches its full development only in contemplative prayer begins in meditation. For Merton, "meditative thought is simply the beginning of a process which leads to interior prayer and is normally supposed to culminate in contemplation and in affective communion with God."[26]

Merton stresses that the distinctive characteristic of religious meditation is that it is a search for truth which springs from love and which seeks to possess the truth not only by knowledge but also by love. The ultimate end of all mental prayer is communion with God: "The identification which we seek to effect in mental prayer is therefore a *conscious realization of the union that is already truly effected between our souls and God by grace . . .*"[27]

Before turning more directly to the prayer of contemplation in Merton's thought, it would be helpful to attempt to clarify some terminology. Although at times Merton seems to equate the two he more often uses the term "contemplative prayer" in a much wider sense than the term "contemplation." In this sense, contemplative prayer would refer more to the "orientation" that one's life of prayer should take. It is more of a method or way of prayer, a general orientation or stance before God and all of life. It involves an emptying process that allows persons to open their hearts to God and to listen to Him in their emptiness; it prepares them to await the word by which God speaks.[28] In Merton's mind, although relatively few would be called to a prayer of contemplation in the strict sense of infused contemplation or mystical prayer, contemplative prayer in the wide sense should characterize every Christian's life of prayer and stance before God.

He particularly recommends this contemplative prayer to his fellow monks. In one of his last books, *Contemplative Prayer*, in which he focuses on monastic prayer, Merton emphasizes what he refers to as a "prayer of the heart" and as a "return to the heart." He writes: "Monastic prayer begins not so much with 'considerations' as with a 'return to the heart,' finding one's deepest center, awakening the profound depths of our being in the presence of God who is the source of our being and our life."[29]   In this "prayer of the heart" we seek God Himself present in the depth of our being. Since it introduces us into deep interior silence so that we learn to experience its power, "it should always be simple, confined to the simplest of acts and often making use of no words and no thoughts at all."[30]   Since we "possess" God in proportion as we realize ourselves to be possessed by Him in the inmost depth of our being, meditation or prayer of the heart is "the active effort we make to keep our hearts open so that we may be enlightened by Him and filled with this realization of our true relation to Him."[31]

# *IV*

Contemplation is at the heart of Merton's thought on prayer. For him, "contemplation is the summit of the Christian life of prayer."[32]   But what is contemplation? This is a question that he frequently sought to clarify in his writings, although he realized that it was ultimately a mystery of our deepest relationship and union with God. He recognized that it could not be taught or clearly explained. It could only be hinted at, suggested, pointed to, symbolized. This he frequently sought to do since he considered it so important. In his early work, *Seeds of Contemplation*, he wrote of contemplation as "the union of our mind and will with God in a supreme act of pure love that is at the same time the highest knowledge of Him as He is in Himself."[33]   It is the highest expression of our intellectual and spiritual life. It is the awareness of the reality of the infinitely abundant Source of life that is God. "It knows the Source, obscurely, inexplicably, but with a certitude that goes beyond reason and simple faith."[34]   Merton goes on to say:

> In other words, then, contemplation reaches out to the knowledge and even to the experience of the transcendent and inexpressible God. It knows God by seeming to touch Him. Or rather it knows Him as if it had been invisibly touched by Him. . . . Touched by Him Who has no hands, but Who is pure Reality and the source of all that is real! Hence contemplation is a sudden gift of awareness, an awakening to the Real within all that is real. A vivid awareness of infinite Being at the roots of our own limited being. An awareness of our contingent reality as received, as a present from God, as a free gift of love.[35]

Merton stresses that contemplation is an inner awakening of a God-intended self, of a genuine center within us which is the counterpart to the divine center calling to us. Since our identity is found in Christ, in being loved by Christ, we should seek, according to Merton, to find that point in the center of our being where we are known and seen by God. Contemplation is getting down to this level and being in God's presence — being known by God and responding as best we can. Contemplation opens persons to themselves; it opens them to God and enables them to embrace everything in God.

If Merton consistently stresses the importance of prayer and contemplation for the individual, he likewise stresses the outward dimensions of all prayer. Recognition of one's union with God must include a recognition of union with all those who live by the same Spirit and are one in Christ. Contemplation is not only grounded in love but also terminates in love. True prayer must lead out to others. Over and over Merton emphasizes: "If we experience God in contemplation, we experience Him not for ourselves alone but also for others."[36] In his mind, true contemplation is essentially communal.

Contemplation must be intimately connected with life and our activity. All prayer, including contemplation, should overflow into a life of fraternal and apostolic charity and a genuine concern and compassion for others:

> In actual fact, true contemplation is inseparable
> from life and from the dynamism of life — which
> includes work, creation, production, fruitfulness,
> and above all *love*. Contemplation is not to be
> thought of as a separate department of life, cut
> off from all man's other interests and superseding
> them. It is the very fullness of a fully integrated life.
> It is the crown of life and of all life's activities.[37]

In Merton's mind there should be no conflict between contemplation and action. However, any genuine apostolic work must be nourished by a spirit of prayer. If we are to be instruments of Christ, we must be united with Christ in love:

Action and contemplation now grow together into
one life and one unity. They become two aspects of
the same thing. Action is charity looking outward to
other men, and contemplation is charity drawn inward to its own divine source. Action is the stream,
and contemplation is the spring. The spring remains
more important than the stream, for the only thing
that really matters is for love to spring up inexhaustibly from the infinite abyss of Christ and of God.[38]

We have seen how a growth in Merton's own prayer led
to a renewed social awareness and concern. This is also
reflected in his later books. For example, he writes in *Life and
Holiness*: "there is no genuine holiness without this dimension of human and social concern. . . . We are obliged to take
an active part in the solution of urgent problems affecting
the whole of society and of our world."[39]   True contemplation in Merton's mind leads inevitably to social concern and
action.[40]

No treatment of prayer in Merton's life and writing
should conclude without some reference to liturgical
prayer, since this type of prayer is normally so much a part
of the life of a monk. Merton's life was no exception and the
community celebration of the Eucharist and the chanting of
the Divine Office in common played a large part in his
monastic life until he made the move to his hermitage in
1965. Since Merton was convinced that Christians do not go
to Christ as isolated individuals but as members of His
Mystical Body, he fully realized the importance of liturgical
prayer and worship and emphasized it in his writings. In his
spirituality there is an intimate relationship between private
prayer and public worship. He frequently sought to show
that there was no necessary conflict between the two types of

prayer and he often described the liturgy as the "school of contemplation."

Although Merton wrote a great deal about liturgical prayer, it is by no means the strongest part of his writings on prayer. With his strong attraction to solitude and solitary prayer, Merton seemed to experience some tension in his own life between corporate and private prayer and this is reflected to some degree in his writings. A certain ambivalence towards the liturgy seemed to be present throughout much of his life, and he does not seem to allow as much scope to the liturgy as others would.[41]

\* \* \* \* \* \* \*

Thomas Merton's extraordinary life ended suddenly in Bangkok, Thailand, in his 54th year. He was accidentally electrocuted by a fan with defective wiring. Death came at a time in his life when his creative mind seemingly had so much more to share with the world. Yet the legacy he has left is an enormously rich one. Many of the seeds he planted have come to fruition in the minds and hearts of his readers. Since his death, his influence has continued to grow and expand under God's grace in an amazing way.

Merton's message continues to be heard. It is a simple message but one that has a special force given the strong witness of his own life of deep faith and persevering prayer. First of all, he reminds us powerfully of the reality of God and the central place God should have in our lives. Secondly, Merton never tires of reminding us of the necessity of prayer, contemplation and solitude. All who seek God sincerely need an element of withdrawal and solitude — time to make the connections in their own lives as they pursue that wholeness that can lie dim and hidden. This is needed so that they can be open to themselves, open to God, and fully alive to the reality of God in the world around them. Finally, Merton continually reminds us of the fullness of the Christian message. We are all called to union with God and to union with one another in the love of Christ.

In his own life Thomas Merton sought God above all things. He tried to penetrate the mystery of God's love in his own life and to be faithful to that mystery as it unfolded. Through the legacy of his life and writings he will no doubt continue to assist others to penetrate the mystery of God's love in their own lives.

---

1   Thomas Merton, *The Seven Storey Mountain* (New York: Signet Books, 1952), p. 112.

2   *Ibid.*, p. 114.

3   Merton writes: ". . . here was a notion of God that was at the same time deep, precise, simple and accurate and, what is more, charged with implications which I could not even begin to appreciate, but which I could at least dimly estimate, even with my own lack of philosophical training." *Ibid.*, p. 170.

4   Merton frequently discusses these two issues in his journal, *The Sign of Jonas* (New York: Image Books, 1956).

5   *The Seven Storey Mountain*, p. 378.

6   Cf. *The Sign of Jonas*, p. 326.

7   This comes through very clearly in the book of essays about Merton, *Thomas Merton, Monk: A Monastic Tribute*, edited by Brother Patrick Hart (New York: Sheed and Ward, 1974).

8   Two of his books that were written prior to Gethsemani were published many years later: *The Secular Journal of Thomas Merton* (1958), and *My Argument with the Gestapo* (1968).

9   Cf. *The Seven Storey Mountain*, p. 400.

10  His abbot of many years, James Fox, O.C.S.O, has some interesting observation in this regard in his essay, "The Spiritual Son," in *Thomas Merton, Monk*, pp. 59-77.

11  *The Sign of Jonas*, p. 97.

12  Cf. *Thomas Merton, Monk*, p. 144.

13  Cf. "Homily," by Flavian Burns, O.C.S.O., in *Thomas Merton, Monk*, pp. 219-220.

14  Cf. Thomas Merton, *Contemplation in a World of Action* (New York: Image Books, 1973), p. 237.

15  For some interesting material about Merton's life as a hermit, see John Howard Griffin's book, *A Hidden Wholeness: The Visual World of Thomas Merton* (Boston: Houghton Mifflin Co., 1970).

16  This statement can be found in the booklet, *The Thomas Merton Reference Studies Center* (Santa Barbara: Unicorn Press, 1971), pp. 14-15. Merton at this time sensed the providential mystery of God's ways. On this occasion his statement was read by Dan Walsh, the person who first told him of the Abbey of Gethsemani. Dan Walsh was an ordained priest at this time.

17  Cf. *Thomas Merton, Monk*, p. 220.

18  Cf. *New Seeds of Contemplation* (New York: New Directions, 1961), xv.

19  These ideas can be found on Merton's tape, "Conference to Sisters on Prayer." They are also developed in the tape put out by Argus Communications, Chicago, IL, "Thomas Merton: Reflections on Prayer."

20  This quote is found in David Steindl-Rast's "Man of Prayer," one of the essays in *Thomas Merton, Monk*, p. 79. The article is based on talks Merton gave to a group at a Trappistine monastery in California at the beginning of his Eastern journey.

21  *Ibid.*, p. 80. Cf. also *A Hidden Wholeness*, p. 2.

22  "Man of Prayer," p. 80.

23  *Ibid.*, p. 81.

24  Cf. Merton's *Seeds of Contemplation* (New York: New Directions, 1949), p. 133.

25  For a discussion of some of these forms in Merton's writings, cf. John F. Teahan, "Meditation and Prayer in Merton's Spirituality," *The American Benedictine Review* (June, 1979), pp. 107-133.

26  Cf. *Merton's Spiritual Direction and Meditation* (Collegeville: The Liturgical Press, 1960), p. 45.

27  *Ibid.*, pp. 66-67.

28  John Higgins develops the meaning of "contemplative prayer" for Merton in his extended study, *Merton's Theology of Prayer* (Spencer: Cistercian Publications, 1971), p. 50 ff. This was later published as an Image Book under the title *Merton on Prayer*.

29  Thomas Merton, *Contemplative Prayer* (New York: Image Books, 1971), p. 30. This was first published under the title, *The Climate of Monastic Prayer*.

30  *Ibid.*, p. 42.

31  *Ibid.*, p. 83.

32  *Contemplative Prayer*, p. 93.

33  *Seeds of Contemplation*, p. 133.

34  *New Seeds of Contemplation*, p. 1.

35  *Ibid.*, pp. 2-3.

36  *New Seeds of Contemplation*, p. 269. Merton also writes: "For contemplation is not ultimately perfect unless it is shared." *Ibid.*, p. 65.

37  Cf. *A Thomas Merton Reader*, Revised Edition. Edited by Thomas O. McDonnell (New York: Image Books, 1974), p. 400.

38  Cf. *No Man is an Island* (New York: Image Books, 1967), p. 65. John Higgins has many good observations on this theme of action and contemplation in his book, *Merton's Theology of Prayer*, p. 70 ff.

39  Thomas Merton, *Life and Holiness* (New York: Image Books, 1964), p. 100.

40  For a fuller development of this theme, cf. James Thomas Baker, *Thomas Merton, Social Critic* (Lexington: University Press of Kentucky, 1971). especially the third chapter entitled, "the Social Ethics of Contemplation," p. 44 ff.

41  For a fuller treatment of liturgical prayer in Merton, cf. Higgins, pp. 75-81, and Teahan, pp. 119-124.

# C.S. LEWIS (1898-1963)

IT IS HARD to believe that Clive Staples Lewis was a single person and not a composite of many talented writers, given the vast and varied quantity of his published works and interests. He was a Classical and English scholar, a theologian, a philosopher, an expert writer of fantasy, science fiction and children's books.

There was, however, a unifying thread to the many sides of C.S. Lewis's talent, and that was his Christian faith. He was a young Oxford don in 1930 when he was converted from atheism to Christianity. For the next 33 years, Lewis placed his many talents at the service of Christianity, becoming one of its most famous exponents to the twentieth century.

In our investigation here, we will look first at Lewis's own conversion experience and then at some of the main aspects of his spirituality and religious thought. Finally we will look at some of his reflections on prayer.

## I

The main source that we have for C.S. Lewis's journey to a religious faith is the account he wrote in 1955 entitled

*Surprised By Joy.* He wrote this partly in answer to the many requests he received to tell how he passed from atheism to Christianity. His encounter with God touched him deeply and so his autobiography is not so much a chronicle of his life as it is an explanation of the way God had persuaded, compelled and conquered him.

As a young boy in Northern Ireland, Lewis received a normal religious education. As he tells us, he was taught the usual things, made to say his prayers, and was in due time taken to church. He recalls that he naturally accepted what he was told but he could not remember feeling much interest in it. His mother's death from cancer when he was nine years old was a blow to the happy family, and the father in his grief drew somewhat apart from Lewis and his older brother, Warren.

Lewis tells us that he became an effective believer for a time at the first boarding school he attended. The instrument was the Anglo-Catholic church to which the students were taken twice every Sunday. The immediate effects were good for him and he writes that he began seriously to pray and to read the Bible and to attempt to obey his conscience.[1] This, however, was not to have any lasting effect and gradually he lost whatever faith he had. By the time he went to study as a young adolescent under the tutelage of W.T. Kirkpatrick ("The Great Knock" as Lewis affectionately called this excellent tutor), Lewis had become a convinced atheist.

Two paths seemed to lead Lewis back as an adult first to theism and ultimately to Christianity. The first was the clear, logical training he received from Kirkpatrick which enabled him to place under logical scrutiny the various philosophic stances he tested and explored. The second and in many ways the more important path for him involved the experience of what Lewis called "Joy." This referred to those fleeting experiences that came unexpectedly to him, triggered by such different things as a beautiful poem, a memory, or a scene. It was a sense of seeing into the heart of things as though a door beyond this universe opened momentarily and then closed suddenly. After giving some personal examples of this experience of Joy, Lewis underlines the quality common to them. For him "it is that of an unsatisfied desire which is itself more desirable than any other satisfaction."[2] They were experiences of intense longing and although the sense of want was acute and even painful, the mere wanting was felt to be somehow a delight. There was for Lewis, too, a peculiar mystery about the object of the desire.

These fleeting revelations of Joy continued off and on over the years for Lewis. Some of his readings played a significant role in this regard. The book *Siegfried and the Twilight of the Gods* was a particularly rich find, and it led to his interest in the musical dramas of Wagner and Norse and Celtic mythology: "Sometimes I can almost think that I was sent back to the false gods there to acquire some capacity for worship against the day when the true God should recall me to Himself."[3]

His reading of George MacDonald's *Phantastes, a faerie Romance* opened up vast new insights. His previous experiences of Joy stayed only long enough to tantalize him and make him long for another such experience. Each visitation of Joy had left the common world momentarily a desert. But this Joy was different, for it somehow transformed the common things of ordinary life: "But now I saw the bright shadow coming out of the book into the real world and resting there, transforming all common things and yet itself unchanged. Or, more accurately, I saw the common things drawn into the bright shadow."[4] Later he spoke of this as the conversion or even baptism of his imagination.

Although his intellect and conscience remained unaffected at that time, their turn would come later with the help of many other books and persons. It was to be a long time before he finally "gave in and admitted that God was God."

His first visit to Oxford was somewhat of an allegorical illustration of this spiritual journey. He went there as he tells us "dreaming spires" and "last enchantments." He got off the train and wandered through the town becoming more and more disappointed and bewildered by what he saw of the succession of mean shops. Only when he seemed to be leaving the town and getting to open country did he turn around. Far away in the distance he saw the beautiful cluster of spires and towers of Oxford. He had come out of the railroad station on the wrong side and had all the time been walking in the wrong direction.

Gradually, Lewis came to realize that the experience of Joy is not an end in itself, but a pointer and a reminder of something else. He came to see that as mortals we are appearances of the Absolute: "In so far as we really are at all . . . we have, so to speak a root in the Absolute, which is the utter reality. And that is why we experience Joy: we yearn, rightly, for that unity which we can never reach except by ceasing to be the separate phenomenal beings called 'we'."[5]   For Lewis, then, Joy was the signpost which showed him that there was something other than a life spent wandering the Oxford road of mean shops. Joy helped him to turn around and see the towers.

These, then, were the two roads that led Lewis back to the religion he had renounced much earlier in his life. The first involved the workings of his logical and penetrating mind, and the second was the experience of Joy, the experience of a yearning whose object was unknown. It was a long and winding process but by the age of thirty he felt God closing in on him. He writes vividly of that moment of reluctant surrender to God's grace one night in his room at Magdalen College:

> You must picture me alone in that room at Magdalen, night after night, feeling, whenever my mind lifted even for a second from my work, the steady, unrelenting approach of Him whom I so earnestly desired not to meet. That which I greatly feared had at last come upon me. In the Trinity Term of 1929 I gave in, and admitted that God was God, and knelt and prayed: perhaps, that night, the most dejected and reluctant convert in all England. I did not then see what is now the most shining and obvious thing; the Divine humility which will accept a convert even on such terms. The Prodigal Son at least walked home on his own feet. But who can duly adore that Love which will open the high gates to a prodigal who is brought in kicking, struggling, resentful, and darting his eyes in every direction for a chance of escape? The words *compelle intrare*, compel them to come in, have been so abused by wicked men that we shudder at them; but, properly understood, they plumb the depth of the Divine mercy. The hardness of God is kinder than the softness of men, and His compulsion is our liberation.[6]

Lewis stresses in his autobiography that the conversion recorded above was to theism, not to Christianity. At that time he knew little about Christ and the Incarnation. He did begin attending his parish church on Sundays and the college chapel on weekdays, for he felt there should be some outward mark of his new faith even though he did not believe at this time in Christianity. What Lewis needed was time to study the New Testament and the central role played by Christ. He struggled particularly to understand the doctrine of the Redemption and the precise way in which Christ's life and death brought about salvation. The day came when he finally found himself convinced that the story of Christ was a true myth: a myth working on us in the same way as the others, but with the tremendous difference that it really happened.[7]

Lewis's final step was taken on an unlikely occasion — a trip to the Whipsnade Zoo one sunny morning with his brother for a picnic lunch. He later wrote of this time:

> When we set out I did not believe that Jesus Christ is the Son of God, and when we reached the zoo I did. Yet I had not exactly spent the journey in thought. Nor in great emotion. 'Emotional' is perhaps the last word we can apply to some of the most important events. It was more like when a man, after long sleep, still lying motionless in bed, becomes aware that he is now awake.[8]

Lewis's entire life after his conversion was spent in the academic circles of Oxford and Cambridge. He was elected a Fellow at Magdalen College as Tutor in English Language and Literature in 1925, and he remained in this position at Oxford for almost thirty years. From 1954 until his death in 1963, he held the new chair of Medieval and Renaissance English at Cambridge University. Externally they were quiet years as he went about his task of tutoring and lecturing, but they were also years of great literary productivity. His first attempts were in the area of poetry, but gradually it was as a prose writer that Lewis became and remains famous. There were his scholarly writings on English literature such as *The Allegory of Love, A Preface to 'Paradise Lost'* and *English*

*Literature in the 16th Century.* His greatest fame was to come, however, from his religious and imaginative writings.

Lewis's conversion to Christianity provided the impetus for much of his writings that followed. His own spiritual journey made him sensitive and sympathetic to nonbelievers, since he knew their problems from personal experience. *The Problem of Pain* appeared in 1940 and it was his first book dealing with a specific religious topic. It was followed over the years by such books as *The Screwtape Letters, Mere Christianity, The Abolition of Man, The Great Divorce, Miracles, Surprised By Joy, Reflections on the Psalms, The Four Loves, A Grief Observed,* and *Letters to Malcolm: Chiefly on Prayer.*

Note should be made of his space trilogy, *Out of the Silent Planet, Perelandra* and *That Hideous Strength,* where Lewis's soaring imagination and Christian sensibility came together in a tale where space itself seems radiated by the presence of the divine. There were also the immensely popular children's stories, the seven books known as *The Chronicles of Narnia.* Finally, any brief account of Lewis's literary productivity should not pass over his great output as a letter writer. He carried on a fruitful apostolate through this medium and he was a pastoral guide and counselor to many who sought his advice.

# *II*

Lewis's conversion experience left him not only a convinced Christian personally but also one who wished to share the fruits of that experience and his own insight with others. With his brilliant mind and his literary talent, he was well equipped to do so, and it was as a Christian apologist that his fame and popularity grew.

The first book resulting from his conversion was a tale entitled *The Pilgrim's Regress* (1933). The subtitle of the book, "An Allegorical Apology For Christianity, Reason, and Romanticism," indicates the main thrust of his concern here and in so much of his subsequent writings. He is searching for a way of looking at experience that will satisfy both the mind and the heart.

The term "romantic rationalist" has often been used in describing C.S. Lewis since the marks of both romanticism and realism are very evident in his life and writings. The romantic element, as we have seen, flowed from his frequent encounters with Joy and his creative imagination that had been nurtured over the years through his vast readings. The rationalism was traceable to the rigorous training in clear thinking that he received from his tutor, W.T. Kirkpatrick.

These two strands, however, did not blend in any automatic way. A catalyst was needed that would be powerful enough to bring these diverse gifts together. Christianity proved to be this catalyst in Lewis's case and both the romantic and rationalist sides of his personality benefited greatly. As Christianity became the unifying force as well as the subtle background for his writings, certain books stressed one of these two aspects. For example, his fiction for both adults and children give large play to his romanticism and lively imagination. On the other hand, such religious works as *Mere Christianity, Miracles* and *The Problem of Pain* show clearly his incisive and logical reasoning. It could also be said that the aspects of rationalism, romanticism and Christianity correspond to the three main genres of his writing: literary criticism, imaginative fiction and Christian apologetics.[9]

Lewis has often been referred to as one of the most important Christian apologists of this century. Austin

Farrer, a close and longtime friend of Lewis, writes insight-
fully of his role as a Christian apologist:

> Lewis was an apologist from temper, from con-
> viction, and from modesty. From temper, for he
> loved an argument. From conviction, being tradi-
> tionally orthodox. From modesty, because he laid no
> claim either to the learning which would have made
> him a theologian or to the grace which would have
> made him a spiritual guide.[10]

Recognizing, too, that rational argument does not create
belief but maintains a climate in which belief may flourish,
he feels that Lewis goes even further and provides a positive
exhibition of the force of Christian ideas morally, imagina-
tively and rationally. The strength of his appeal lies in the
manysidedness of his work. "The Lewis who has cleared the
ground by his controversial argument admits his readers to
a mental world of great richness, great vigor and clarity, and
in every corner illuminated by his Christian belief."[11]   The
reader is admitted, indeed, into the Christian world of C.S.
Lewis.

It is in the area Lewis refers to as "Mere Christianity" that
we find his most important contribution as a Christian
apologist. In 1941, he was invited by the Director of Religious Broadcasting for the BBC to give a series of radio
broadcasts. The invitation was attractive to him, for he had
long regarded England as part of that "post-Christian"
world in need of a special missionary technique — "one
which must take into account the fact that many people were
under the impression that they had rejected Christianity
when in truth, they had never had it."[12]

Lewis knew from the beginning the methodology he
wanted to employ, for he believed very firmly that people

must be convinced of their real limitations and their capacity to sin before they will welcome the remedy. Thus he sought to challenge the conscience of those who feel no guilt and then present the gospel message in a way they could understand.

The complete broadcasts consisted of four fifteen-minute talks entitled "Right and Wrong: A Clue to the Meaning of the Universe"; five talks on "What Christians Believe"; eight talks on "Christian Behavior"; and a last set of seven talks entitled "Beyond Personality: The Christian View of God." The presentation proved to be enormously popular and later they were all collected and published under the title *Mere Christianity*.

In these broadcasts Lewis sought to explain as clearly and concisely as possible what Christianity is about. He wanted to focus on the essentials of the Christian faith and avoid anything that was peculiar to himself or unacceptable to the main body of Christians. It was essential or "mere" Christianity that he wanted to expound; he wanted, as he tells us himself, "to explain and defend the belief that has been common to nearly all Christians at all times."[13]   It was a small-scale presentation of Christian theology that he brought forth.

There is no question that Lewis was very successful in this endeavor, for he brought his great gifts of a brilliant and logical mind to the task. Few can surpass the clarity of his thinking and his capacity to encapsulate a great deal of information into a few words.

Lewis never claimed to be doing anything original or unique in this area, and yet it has often been said that Lewis is nowhere more original than in this particular work. Basically his originality is found in the simple direct-ness and the freshness of his approach and presentation of the basics of the Christian message. As his biographers conclude:

> The interesting thing, the thing which cannot be too heavily emphasized in any study of the man or his works, is that though the setting of some of his works are strange and wonderful, his greatest claim to "originality" rests in his total espousal of what Screwtape wryly denounced as the "Same Old Thing" and Richard Baxter (from whom Lewis borrowed the term) called "mere Christianity."[14]

In this connection it is interesting to recall something Lewis wrote in *Mere Christianity*. Although he was writing in another context, it does shed some light on this question:

> Even in literature and art, no man who bothers about originality will ever be original: whereas if you simply try to tell the truth (without caring twopence how often it has been told before) you will, nine times out of ten, become original without ever having noticed it. The principle runs through all life from top to bottom. Give up yourself and you will find your real self.[15]

## III

Let us turn now to some of C.S. Lewis's reflections on prayer. Again in this area, he is careful not to put himself forward as any authority on the subject. His stance is that of a believer who is convinced of the importance of prayer in his own life and in the life of every Christian. He seeks to share some of his own insights as well as some of the problems and difficulties connected with prayer. The main source for these ideas is his posthumously published *Letters to Malcolm: Chiefly on Prayer*. His reflections are expressed in the form of informal, chatty letters to a friend and the reader is allowed to listen in as two ordinary laymen discuss various practical and speculative issues connected with prayer.

Lewis is primarily interested in private prayer in these letters. What he has to say about corporate prayer he says early and somewhat briefly and pungently. He is very unsympathetic to novelties which he feels easily distract from the main point of worship. His own liturgical position really boils down to an entreaty for permanence and uniformity with changes occurring only gradually and imperceptibly. He writes: "Already our liturgy is one of the few remaining elements of unity in our hideously divided Church. The good to be done by revision needs to be very great and very certain before we throw that away."[16]

Lewis's approach to personal prayer is very practical. It is rooted in his own experience of prayer and that of others who consulted him on this topic. He is down to earth in his approach and does not hesitate to tackle common problems and difficulties that arise. His remarks in this area are marked by an openness and tolerance for individual differences and preferences. For example, in discussing using one's own words in prayer and using ready-made prayers, he comments on Rose Macaulay's continual search for different set prayers. Although surprised, he is in no way critical of this practice. He doesn't doubt that her method is the right one for her although it would not be for himself.

Although he thinks one's practice changes and ought to change, Lewis's preference at the time of writing is to make his own words the staple while introducing a modicum of the ready-made. The homemade staples are the best for him, for he recognizes that "no other creature is identical with me; no other situation identical with mine. Indeed, I myself and my situation are in continual change."[17] Yet he also admits that the ready-made prayers are beneficial for himself, for they keep him in touch with "sound doctrine," and remind him of what things he ought to ask, and not to overlook the things that should not be overlooked. Finally, recognizing the paradox between God's proximity and distance, he finds that set prayers provide an element of the ceremonial.

Lewis also has some suggestions as to time, place, posture, etc., in which he shares his own preferences and opinions. Regarding the time of prayer, he strongly urges that we do not reserve our chief prayer for bed-time, for he feels it is the worst possible hour for any action which needs concentration. He confesses that he finds it difficult to pray in church since he is distracted by other people. He also recognizes the importance of the body in prayer and the importance of kneeling, but he adds: "The relevant point is that kneeling does matter, but other things matter even more. A concentrated mind and a sitting body make for better prayer than a kneeling body and a mind half asleep."[18]

In keeping with his tendency not to shy away from difficult problems, Lewis does not hesitate to zero in on some of the difficulties surrounding petitionary prayer. His logical thinking again comes to the fore as he attempts to answer some of the objections commonly associated with this type of prayer, such as: "If God is omniscient, why is it necessary to make known our needs to him?" Lewis offered the following:

> We are always completely, and therefore equally, known to God. That is our destiny whether we like it

or not. But though this knowledge never varies, the quality of our being known can. . . . Ordinarily, to be known by God is to be, for this purpose, in the category of things. We are, like earthworms, cabbages, nebulae, objects of Divine knowledge. But when we    (a) become aware of the fact — the present fact, not the generalisation — and    (b) assent with all our will to be so known, then we treat ourselves, in relation to God, not as things, but as persons. We have unveiled. Not that any veil could have baffled His sight. The change is in us. The passive changes to the active. Instead of merely being known, we show, we tell, we offer ourselves to view.[19]

Thus, Lewis raises it to a question of a personal relationship with God:

To put ourselves thus on a personal footing with God could, in itself and without warrant, be nothing but presumption and illusion. But we are taught that it is not; that it is God who gives us that footing. For it is by the Holy Spirit that we cry 'Father'. By unveiling, by confessing our sins and 'making known' our requests, we assume the high rank of persons before Him. And he, descending, becomes Person to us.[20]

There is no question in Lewis's mind of the important place petitionary prayer should play in one's faith. The New Testament clearly recommends it to us both by precept and example. Christ's prayer in Gethsemani is but one example. His conclusion is direct and to the point in this matter:

Whatever the theoretical difficulties are, we must
continue to make requests of God. And on this point
we can get no help from those who keep on reminding us that this is the lowest and least essential kind
of prayer. They may be right, but so what?[21]

Lewis acknowledges that often petitionary prayer pre-
dominates in a time of crisis and anxiety similar in some
respects to Jesus' prayer in Gethsemani. He does not agree,
however, with those who feel guilty about these anxieties
and regard them as a defect of faith. In his mind they are
afflictions that can be our share in the Passion of Christ. The
prayer in Gethsemani shows that the anxiety which precedes
prayer is equally God's will and equally part of our human
destiny. Jesus experienced it and the servant is not greater
than the master.[22]

In the course of his reflections on petitionary prayer,
Lewis addresses himself to the question of the causality of
prayer, asking if prayer, or some prayers, are actual causes.
He recognizes the inadequacy of applying strictly causal
thinking to the relationship between God and human
persons. And yet he would want to allow for some influence
on the part of creatures for he writes:

I would rather say that from before all worlds
His providential and creative act (for they are all
one) takes into account all the situations produced by
the acts of His creatures. And if he takes our sins into
account, why not our petitions?[23]

Lewis would prefer, then, to speak about our prayers
being "taken into account" rather than in terms of a causal
connection:

To think of our prayers as just 'causes' would suggest that the whole importance of petitionary prayer lay in the achievement of the thing asked for. But really, for our spiritual life as a whole, the 'being taken into account', or 'considered', matters more than the being granted. Religious people don't talk about the 'results' of prayer; they talk of its being 'answered' or 'heard.'[24]

Lewis focuses on another difficulty regarding petitionary prayer. It deals with the promises made in the New Testament that what we pray for with faith we shall receive. Mark 12:24 would be one such example. He wonders how this promise is to be reconciled with (a) the observed fact that petitions are not always granted, and (b) the universally accepted view, following Jesus' prayer in Gethsemane, that we should ask everything with the reservation — "If it be thy will." If a person envisages a refusal as possible, how can one have at the same time a perfect confidence that what is asked will not be refused?

Lewis hints at some possible responses to the difficulty. First, he concludes that such promises about prayer with faith refer to a degree of faith which most believers never experience. He hopes that a far inferior degree is acceptable to God, even the kind that says, "Help thou my unbelief." Secondly, he makes the distinction between the prayer of the suitor and the prayer of the servant as he wonders how or why such faith occurs sometimes but not always. His own opinion is that it occurs only when the one who prays does so as God's fellow worker asking what is needed for the joint work. It is the prayer of the prophet, the apostle, the missionary, the healer that is made with this confidence. On the other hand, the suitor is praying on his own behalf. Lewis concludes:

... it would be no true faith — it would be idle
presumption — for us, who are habitually suitors
and do not often rise to the level of servants, to
imagine that we shall have any assurance which is
not an illusion — or correct only by accident — about
the events of our prayers. Our struggle is, isn't it? —
to achieve and retain faith on a lower level. To
believe that, whether He can grant them or not, God
will listen to our prayers, will take them into account.
Even to go on believing that there is a Listener at all.
For as the situation grows more and more desperate,
the grisly fears intrude. Are we only talking to
ourselves in an empty universe? The silence is often
so emphatic. And we have prayed so much already.[25]

Lewis returns in a later letter to this same fear that
prayer is just a soliloquoy. He does not hesitate to speak of
prayer as a soliloquoy, but he uses it in the sense of God
speaking to Himself through the prayer of the human
person. It is the Holy Spirit speaking in us. If one wonders
why God should speak to Himself through persons, Lewis
answers that it is God's way to work through His creatures:

Creation seems to be delegation through and
through. He will do nothing simply of Himself
which can be done by creatures. I suppose this is
because He is a giver. And He has nothing to give
but Himself. And He has nothing to give
— in a sense, and on varying levels to be Himself —
through the things He has made.[26]

Lewis also has some insightful reflections on what can be
referred to as sensing God's presence in all things. He in no
way wants to minimize specifically holy places and things

and days, for as he writes, "without these focal points or reminders, the belief that all is holy and 'big with God' will dwindle into a mere sentiment."[27]   Yet he also wants to stress God's presence in creatures — in a world that is "crowded with Him":

> But in order to find God it is perhaps not always necessary to leave the creatures behind. We may ignore, but we can nowhere evade, the presence of God. The world is crowded with Him. He walks everywhere *incognito*. And the *incognito* is not always hard to penetrate. The real labour is to remember, to attend. In fact, to come awake. Still more, to remain awake.[28]

Lewis stresses that the ordinary pleasures of our lives are excellent places to become aware of God and His glory. In giving praise and adoration to God, we should "begin where we are." Ordinary experiences of life are excellent starting points. For example, the experience of splashing one's hot face and hands in a little waterfall can be an exposition of God's glory. Such pleasures for Lewis are shafts of His glory as it strikes our sensibility. He writes very simply and beautifully of such experiences:

> One must learn to walk before one can run. So here, We — or at least I — shall not be able to adore God on the highest occasions if we have learned no habit of doing so on the lowest. At best, our faith and reason will tell us that He is adorable, but we shall not have found Him so, not have 'tasted and seen'. Any patch of sunlight in a wood will show you something about the sun which you could never get from read-

ing books on astronomy. These pure and spontane-
ous pleasures are 'patches of Godlight' in the woods
of our experience.[29]

\* \* \* \* \* \* \*

Lewis remarks in one place that the prayer that should
precede all prayer is, "May it be the real I who speaks. May it
be the real Thou that I speak to."[30]    This same desire for
sincerity, authenticity and insight marks so much of C.S.
Lewis's life and writings. For him it is a matter of being
touched by God and seeing beyond the present world. It is a
matter of continually reawakened awareness to the reality of
God in our lives and our need to respond simply and completely. We might conclude with these words from Lewis:

> Only God Himself can let the bucket down to the
> depths in us. And, on the other side, He must con-
> stantly work as the iconoclast. Every idea of Him we
> form, He must in mercy shatter. The most blessed
> result of prayer would be to rise thinking, 'But I
> never knew before. I never dreamed. . . .'[31]

---

1  C.S. Lewis, *Surprised By Joy* (London: Collins, Fontana Books, 1959), p. 33.

2  *Ibid.*, p. 20.

3  *Ibid.*, p. 65.

4  *Ibid.*, p. 146.

5  *Ibid.*, p. 177.

6  *Ibid.*, pp. 182-183.

7  Roger Lancelyn Green and Walter Hooper, *C.S. Lewis, A Biography* (New York:
   Harcourt Brace Jovanovich, Harvest Books, 1976), p. 118.

8  *Surprised By Joy*, p. 189.

9  Cf. Peter Kreeft, *C.S. Lewis: A Critical Essay* (Grand Rapids: Eerdmans, 1969),
   p. 13.

10 Austin Farrer, "The Christian Apologist," *Light on C.S. Lewis*, ed. by Jocelyn Gibb (New York: Harcourt, Brace, 1965), p. 24.
11 *Ibid.*, p. 26.
12 Green and Hooper, p. 202.
13 C.S. Lewis, *Mere Christianity* (New York: Macmillan, 1960), p. 6.
14 Green and Hooper, p. 211.
15 *Mere Christianity*, p. 190.
16 C.S. Lewis, *Letters to Malcolm: Chiefly on Prayer* (London: Fontana, 1966), p. 8.
17 *Ibid.*, p. 14.
18 *Ibid.*, p. 19.
19 *Ibid.*, p. 22.
20 *Ibid.*, pp. 22-23.
21 *Ibid.*, pp. 38-39.
22 *Ibid.*, p. 45.
23 *Ibid.*, p. 53.
24 *Ibid.*, p. 55.
25 *Ibid.*, p. 64.
26 *Ibid.*, p. 73.
27 *Ibid.*, p. 76.
28 *Ibid.*, pp.76-77.
29 *Ibid.*, p. 93.
30 *Ibid.*, p. 83.
31 *Ibid.*, p. 84.

# Pierre Teilhard
# DE CHARDIN (1881-1955)

AS A JESUIT PRIEST, scientist and writer Teilhard de Chardin has had much influence upon various areas of Christian theology in the twentieth century. Many have noted, however, that his greatest contribution seems to be the careful development over the course of his life of a rich spirituality of the Christian's role in the world centered on the Risen Christ.[1]

It is important to note here at the outset that Teilhard's spiritual writings are not so much a system as they are a sharing in his own personal vision. His writings flow from his reflections on his own life and his own personal spirituality.[2] Throughout his life he sought for the absolute. He sought to make known what was hidden. His search for God and his love of the earth blossomed together into a vocation to be both a Jesuit priest and a geologist. He was, indeed, a mystic who sought to disclose the presence of Christ in all things.

Teilhard was so caught up in this vision that his overriding desire in all his writings was to help others "to see." He sought intensely and passionately to assist others to come to an understanding of the vision which he himself saw so vividly. He was a missionary and an apostle who sought energetically and insistently to unveil the presence of God in the world through the Risen Christ. He sought to proclaim Christ in all His fullness.

Since Teilhard had a personal vision that he wanted to articulate and propose to others, he was a pioneer in many ways. In his writings he was forging new paths and new horizons. We should not be surprised, then, to find Teilhard's life marked by a certain amount of controversy and misunderstanding. Because of his writings, he encountered a good measure of suspicion and opposition, particularly from his religious superiors, and this caused him much pain and anguish. One must also keep in mind the complexity of his thought and the newness of his language that made some aspects of his thought difficult to comprehend. Still, it has long been recognized that there is a power in his words that often awakens an immediate rapport, and there is much that seems to answer a profound need of our age. Any attempt, then, to understand and appreciate his vision can be very rewarding.[3]

In this chapter we will focus first on an overview of Teilhard's life since this should help to put his vision and writings in perspective. Secondly, there will be a consideration of the future orientation of his thought (his eschatology). This will be followed by a treatment of the centrality of Christ in all his writings with special reference to his spirituality of the Cross. Finally, the implications of his vision for Christian living will be considered, that is, his mysticism of Christian involvement in the world.

# I

Pierre Teilhard de Chardin was born on May 1, 1881, in Sarcenat, France, the fourth of eleven children in a family of deep faith. Even as a young boy, his interest in natural history was evident, and he spent long hours investigating the stones and rocks found on his family's land and the surrounding region. He studied at the Jesuit college of Mongré as a young man and then entered the Jesuit novitiate in Aix-en-Provence in 1899. After his philosophical studies on the island of Jersey (1902-1905), he taught college chemistry and physics as a Jesuit scholastic in Cairo (1905-1908), and then studied theology in preparation for the priesthood in Hastings, England (1908-1912). Each of these regions played a part in fostering his interests in geology and paleontology and also afforded him the opportunity to set down his developing ideas in numerous letters to friends and loved ones.

After his ordination to the priesthood, Teilhard began graduate studies in geology at Paris. With the outbreak of the First World War, however, these studies were interrupted, and Teilhard was called up for military service in 1914 and served as a stretcher-bearer at the front for the duration of the war. His experiences of war brought him face to face with the ultimate realities of life, and this played a great part in the development of his own religious and philosophical thinking. Important writings flow from this period that contain the seeds of his thought that would be developed more fully at a later date. His letters to his cousin, Marguerite Teilhard de Chambon were later collected and published under the title *The Making of a Mind*, and there were various religious and philosophical essays that were later published as *Writings in Time of War*.[4]

The conclusion of the war allowed him to return to Paris to resume his doctoral studies. He received his doctorate in 1922 and then taught geology at the Institut Catholique in Paris for the next three years. It was also a time of field trips to China and continued research and writing.

Difficulties over some of his writings, particularly an essay he had written regarding the Genesis account of the Fall, broke out in 1925. It led his religious superiors to require that he resign his teaching position at Paris and take on a new assignment in China. China would be the principal area of his work for the next twenty years. During this time he became one of the great specialists of East Asian geology and paleontology and he continued to develop his thought through his extensive writings.

The winter of 1926-1927 saw the birth of his important spiritual work, *The Divine Milieu*[5]. Then from 1938-1940 he wrote his major work, *The Phenomenon of Man*, a study that would establish his reputation even more when finally published.[6]   It is a work that bridges the span of evolution from the distant past to future developments with an explicitly Christian focus.

In May of 1946, Teilhard returned to Paris and began lecturing again. Problems with the publication of *The Phenomenon of Man* came to a head in 1948 and he was unable to receive permission from religious superiors to publish the work. He was also denied permission to accept a chair in paleontology at the College de France. In 1951, Teilhard became a scientific associate to the Viking Fund (later the Werner Gren Foundation) for the support and encouragement of anthropological studies. He remained in this position until his death, with the United States as the base of operation for his scholarly work and travel. Death came suddenly to Teilhard on Easter Sunday, March 15, 1955, after suffering a heart attack in New York City. It was fitting in many ways that he went to meet the Risen Christ he had always sought to serve and make known on Easter Sunday.

# *II*

Teilhard was convinced that the biggest problem facing the contemporary Christian was the difficulty of reconciling faith in God and faith in the world. There often seemed to be a conflict between believing in God and believing in human activity and progress. On the one hand there is an upward impulse towards a faith in God and a love of God, accompanied by a certain detachment from the world. On the other hand, there is a forward impulse toward involvement in the world and towards human activity and progress. Thus, the Christian seems to be caught between two opposite movements. This was the basic problem for Teilhard and what he sought to share was a world vision that would resolve the apparent conflict.

For Teilhard there could be a compatibility between religion and science, between a faith in God and a faith in the world. He was convinced that a person could be fully Christian and fully human at the same time, united with God through the world. All this is made possible through the Risen Christ who is at the center of the world. For Teilhard faith in the world means faith in Jesus Christ, because the Lordship of Christ embraces the whole world. The world is important because it belongs to the Lordship of Christ. Since it is Jesus Christ who makes the synthesis between God and the world possible, a personal relationship with the Risen Christ is at the heart of Teilhard's spirituality.

In Teilhard's overall world view there are three distinct phases or steps that form the important elements in his religious thought. First there is his theory of evolution. In this theory there is a strong focus on the future, for he is interested not so much in how things began but in how they will end. He finds all things moving purposefully towards a focal point, the last moment of human history. He calls this point Omega, after the last letter in the Greek alphabet. It is within this evolutionary world view that Teilhard situates his Christology, the second main element of his thought, for he identifies the Omega Point with the Second Coming of Christ at the end of the world. Finally, on his Christology he builds a kind of mysticism of involvement in the world. Since the Risen Lord is the focal point of the world in evolution, all human effort carried out in Jesus has great value.

Let us focus more fully now on each of these phases of his thought beginning with his evolutionary theory and eschatology. There will be a certain amount of overlapping since all of these phases are intimately connected with one another and together form one world view. Teilhard continued to develop each of these aspects simultaneously throughout his life, so we cannot speak of any chronological development from one aspect to the next.

## Evolutionary Theory and Eschatology

Teilhard's theory of evolution is, of course, a foundational aspect of his religious and philosophical thought. As noted earlier, his main focus of interest is on the future. He is looking ahead to the future and to the final outcome of all things. He wants to know where the world is going and where humanity is headed. His theory of evolution, then, is aimed at endings, not beginnings.

The whole evolutionary process for Teilhard is not unordered or unstructured. It has a definite purpose and direction in all its movement, and that direction is towards greater degrees of organization and complexity. With this increasing organization comes greater consciousness and greater awareness. The most highly organized being on earth is the human person and thus the most conscious.

Evolution, however, does not stop with the human person. With the human person, the process of evolution becomes conscious of itself and takes the form of human progress. Human society in its own evolution follows the same laws of complexity, organization and consciousness.

Teilhard recognizes that human persons are finite and so he speaks of a point beyond which they cannot evolve. There will be a final point to this entire process of evolution and a final stage of all human activity and history. This is what Teilhard calls the Omega Point. He uses the image of a cone lying on its side to help bring out this movement towards a definite point, with the top of the cone signifying the Omega Point. And as noted already, he equates Omega with the Second Coming of Christ at the final moment of world history. Thus, the Parousia or the Second Coming of Christ is the central Christian mystery in his theology which has such a strong eschatological focus.

Teilhard's religious thought, then, is definitely future oriented with a view of the world that stresses evolution, progress and building towards the future. Without going into all of Teilhard's somewhat complicated terminology, we might say simply that in light of the Christian teaching on creation and Incarnation. Teilhard looked upon the entire evolution of the cosmos (cosmogenesis) as a true Christogenesis, the becoming of the Cosmic Christ. He sees the universe converging in an historical evolutionary process towards its ultimate goal, Jesus Christ, and towards the final reconciliation of all things in Him.

In this entire process, love will play a major role because it is the key source of energy that carries humanity into the future. Love binds the individual elements in the universe to each other and to the universe's personal Center. Teilhard is convinced that as a "phylum of love" Christianity has a major role in the universe's evolution.

*Teilhard's Christology*

It is within this evolutionary context of the world in progress that Teilhard situates his theology of Christ. As noted earlier, he identifies the Omega Point, the final point of all human effort and progress, with the Risen Jesus. It is Jesus Christ who is at the center of the world. He is the principle of unity who integrates our faith in the world and our faith in God.

There is, to be sure, a very strong apocalyptic dimension to Teilhard's Christology with his identification of the Omega Point with the Second Coming of Jesus at the end of the world. For Teilhard, the Risen Jesus is the Omega Point, and in stressing this, he echoes the words from the Book of Revelation, "I am the Alpha and the Omega."

In developing his thought on Christ, Teilhard is thus influenced by the Book of Revelation. But he is influenced even more by the theology of St. Paul, especially as it is contained in the letters to the Ephesians and to the Colossians. For example, he is indebted to Paul's doctrine of the recapitulation of all things in Jesus Risen as developed in Colossians 1:15-20. Paul here stresses that Christ is the head of all creation who holds all things in unity, "the image of the unseen God, the first born of all creation, for in Him were created all things in heaven and on earth." Teilhard builds upon this Christology of St. Paul, reinterpreting it in light of his own theory of the world in evolution.[7]

Like the Christ of St. Paul, the Christ of Teilhard is often referred to as the Cosmic Christ because He is Lord of the whole Cosmos. It is the universal and Cosmic Christ that holds all things together for Teilhard. Although he thus emphasizes the cosmic, universal Christ, it should be stressed that he never lost sight of the historical Jesus. The Jesus of the Cosmos is not an archetype or something impersonal. The Cosmic Christ is the same Jesus who was born in Bethlehem, and who suffered, died and rose from the dead.

Although Teilhard focuses forcefully on Christ as Lord of the whole cosmos who will come in power at the end of the world to reconcile all things, he never wants it to be forgotten that Christ is already present in His power and acting on the world and our lives very profoundly at the present time. The Risen Christ breaks into the present out of the ultimate future.

*A Personal Relationship with Christ*

It is important to realize that the basis of Teilhard's writings about the centrality of Christ was his own personal relationship with Jesus Christ. Teilhard personally lived out the problem of reconciling his life as a scientist and his life as a religious priest as well as his love for God and his love for science. But he lived more its solution, for he found the synthesis of both of these deep attractions in the Risen Christ. Christ for him was the principle of unity.

Teilhard's own personal prayer and the notes he left from his annual retreats give us a good idea of his own relationship with Christ. As a Jesuit priest he was, of course, steeped in the spirituality of the *Spiritual Exercises* of St. Ignatius of Loyola. The last exercise of prayer known as "The Contemplation to Attain the Love of God" had a special attraction for him. Basically, it is a prayer to find God in all things so that the retreatant may love and serve Him in all things. As one writer aptly describes it: "The reflections of the meditation aim at deepening the appreciation of the presence, the goodness, and the love of God in everything that exists; everything in the retreatant's life is viewed as a gift from God in which God himself is present for the retreatant, acting and working for him out of love."[8]  One can readily see why such a vision of God's love and presence in the world would appeal to Teilhard so strongly.

Teilhard expresses the spirit of this contemplation in a very beautiful prayer that he composed during the First World War when he was in military service. It sums up very well the centrality of Christ in his own life and his own world vision.

> Lord Jesus Christ, you truly contain within your gentleness, within your humanity, all the unyielding immensity and grandeur of the world.
>
> You are the Center at which all things meet and which stretches out over all things so as to draw them back into itself; I love you for the extensions of your body and soul to the farthest corners of creation through grace, through life, and through matter.
>
> Lord Jesus, you who are as gentle as the human heart, as fiery as the forces of nature, as intimate as life itself, you in whom I can melt away and with whom I must have mastery and freedom; I love you as a world, as *this* world which has captivated my heart. . . .
>
> Lord Jesus, you are the center towards which all things are moving.[9]

A second source of Teilhard's personal relationship with Christ can be found in his own devotion to the Sacred Heart. Evidence of this can be found in his private journals and retreat notes. Teilhard writes in one of these journals:

Although I never really analysed it before, it is in the
Sacred Heart that the conjunction of the Divine and
the cosmic has taken place. . . . There lies the power
that, from the beginning, has attracted me and conquered me. . . . All the later development of my
interior life has been nothing other than *the evolution
of that seed.*[10]

It is necessary also to see in this context the importance
of the Eucharist for Teilhard. Although Christ is the focal
point towards which the whole world is headed, the same
Risen Jesus is present now in the midst of ongoing history.
He is present in and through the Eucharist. In his treatment
of the Eucharist, Teilhard stresses the love of Christ present
in and radiating out from the Eucharist, and the significance
of that love for the individual Christian and for the progress
of the Christian community and of human society as a
whole.

The Eucharist joins us physically more closely to Christ
and to the rest of the faithful in a growing world unity.
There is a sense in which the words of the priest, "This is My
Body," extend outwards to the whole universe. The words
of consecration fall not only upon the sacrificial bread and
wine but upon the whole world for, in an extended and
secondary sense, the matter of the sacrament of the
Eucharist is the world itself. For Teilhard, the center of
Christ's personal energy is situated in the Host, but "the
Host is like a blazing hearth from which flames spread their
radiance."[11]

Teilhard develops these ideas in his long and beautiful
prayer, "The Mass on the World." This was a prayer he was
fond of using when he was on geological expeditions and
unable to celebrate Mass each day. In this prayer he
eloquently proclaims his faith in the radiating power of the

Eucharist and the presence of the Universal Christ in the world. His opening words cry out:

> Since once again, Lord — though this time not in the forests of the Aisne but in the steppes of Asia — I have neither bread, nor wine, nor altar, I will raise myself beyond these symbols, up to the pure majesty of the real itself; I, your priest, will make the whole earth my altar and on it will offer you all the labours and sufferings of the world.[12]

*Christian Involvement in the World*

On his theory of evolution and his Christology, Teilhard builds a mysticism of involvement in the world. Since Christ is the focal point of a world in evolution, all human activity carried out in Christ has great significance and value. Christians are called to center their lives on Jesus Christ. They are called to build their lives around Him, integrating all relationships into one central relationship with Him. For Teilhard, a personal union with Jesus Christ is central to Christian holiness. Yet the direction of this holiness and union with Christ is not away from matter or the world or human activity, but directly into all this toward the Risen Christ. The Christian is called to cooperate with God's plan to unite progressively all things in Christ.

Teilhard stresses the value and importance of human activity in his spiritual classic, *The Divine Milieu*. This stress is intimately connected with his vision of the reconciliation of all things in Christ. Christ's Second Coming will be the terminal point of all human evolution, and the Parousia will mark the transformation of all things in Christ. Since nothing that is truly constructive will be lost at the Parousia, human activity has a permanent value, for it contributes to building the world towards its final transformation in Christ.

Teilhard understood the evolution of the world towards the Parousia as the expression of God's continuous creation that is directed towards the fullness of the Pleroma. Again, it is in this context that human activity takes on such value. Human persons are called upon to cooperate with God in building up the world towards the final transformation. They are called to adhere to God's continuously creative action in the gradual formation of the Pleroma.[13]

Human endeavor, then, is a participation in God's creative activity. Teilhard writes: "To begin with, in action I adhere to the creative power of God: I coincide with it; I become not only its instrument but its living extension."[14] Since for Teilhard "God is inexhaustibly attainable in the totality of our action," communion with God comes through our human activity.

In Teilhard's vision, then, God does not stand aloof from the world. On the contrary, He has chosen to involve Himself deeply and thoroughly in the world. He is not apart from the world we see, touch, hear, smell and taste about us. He awaits us every instant in our action, in the work of the moment. For Teilhard there is a sense "in which he is at the tip of my pen, my spade, my brush, my needle — of my heart and of my thought."[15]   Teilhard writes with conviction:

> To repeat: by virtue of the Creation and, still more, of the incarnation, *nothing* here below is *profane* for those who know how to see. On the contrary, everything is sacred to the men who can distinguish that portion of chosen being which is subject to Christ's drawing power in the process of consummation.

> Try, with God's help, to perceive the connection —
> even physical and natural — which binds your labor
> with the building of the kingdom of heaven.[16]

What we do, then, is important, for it is a cooperation with God creating. Human activity has a religious value, and Christians have the right and duty to involve themselves wholeheartedly in the things of the earth. Teilhard's mystical seeking of God in all things stresses that all of human life can be sanctified. Through our work and action and the developing of our talents, we can find God and touch God in all things. For Teilhard, God can be served and worshipped in giving ourselves to creative activity, joining that activity to God to build a better world.

## Spirituality of the Cross

Closely connected with Teilhard's spirituality of Christian involvement in the world is his stress on the place of the Cross in the life of the Christian. His spirituality is, as we have seen, a theology of the Christian life as it is to be lived in this world at the present time. Although Christ is now risen, the Christian who is following Him in this world at the present time is, as Christ was, in the existential structure of the Cross. The Cross, then, is central to his spirituality.

For Teilhard, Christ's redemptive death has two aspects. The first aspect focuses on Christ's redemptive work of the Cross as reparation for sinful disorders in the world. The second aspect focuses on the Cross as the means of reconciliation. In the development of his own spirituality of the Cross, Teilhard will stress this second aspect of reconciliation.

By his death, Jesus reconciled, in principle and in a way that is being worked out in history, all things in Himself. The Cross is a work of unification because, for Teilhard, "Christ is he who structurally in himself, and for all of us, overcame the resistance to unification offered by the multiple resistance to the rise of the spirit inherent in matter." For Teilhard, "the complete and definitive meaning of redemption is no longer only to expiate; it is to surmount and conquer."[17]

Thus, Teilhard sees the Cross as the symbol of progress. It is now the symbol "not merely of the dark retrogressive side of the universe in genesis, but also, and even more, of its triumphant and luminous side." The Cross is "the symbol of progress and victory won through mistakes, disappointments and hard work."[18]

Teilhard's ascetical teaching is the translation into practical terms of what the Cross symbolizes. In *The Divine Milieu*, he devotes a section to the developing of his reflections on the nature of Christian asceticism.[19]　He speaks of three phases or stages of development. If human persons are to be fully themselves and fully alive, they must (1) be centered upon themselves; (2) be "de-centered" upon "the other"; and (3) be "super-centered" upon a being greater than themselves.

First, there is *centration*. It is the lifelong process of growing as a person, becoming more unified as a person, and moving towards Christian maturity. It is the process of being oneself as completely as possible. For Teilhard "it is a truly Christian duty to grow, even in the eyes of men, and to make one's talents bear fruit, even though they be natural."[20]

Secondly, there is *decentration*, which means for Teilhard that "we cannot reach our own ultimate without emerging from ourselves by uniting ourselves with others."[21] *Decentration* expresses for Teilhard the gospel message of renunciation, of losing oneself for the sake of the kingdom so as to find oneself. He stresses that we must rise above the elementary temptation and illusion that personal growth comes only from a selfish and egotistical stance, and see that we grow only by emerging from ourselves and uniting with others.

*Centration* and *decentration* are two phases of the one process for Teilhard. In the general rhythm of Christian life, development and renunciation, attachment and detachment go together. They harmonize together like the inward and outward breathing in the movement of the lungs. They serve as a springboard to the third phase of the dialectic movement of Christian perfection, *surcentration.* This is the stage of surrender and the attaching of our lives to one who is greater than ourselves. It is the phase of union with God, of being centered not on ourselves but on Christ.[22]　As Fr. Faricy succinctly summarizes this process:

> *Centration, decentration, surcentration* are, of course, the categories of the paschal mystery: life, death, resurrection. Just as the life of Jesus was a building towards the final decentration which was his death on the cross and was a passage to the risen life, so too the Christian's life is a continuous building and a fragmenting and a coming apart in order to come together again less centered on self and more centered on Jesus Christ.[23]

Teilhard looks upon his spirituality of the Cross, then, not as an asceticism of flight from the world, but as a program of involvement in the world. The Cross is the way that leads to resurrection. In his mind, then, there is no conflict between the Cross and involvement in the world, for the two go together by nature of the very structure of reality.

\*   \*   \*   \*   \*   \*   \*

At the beginning of the third part of *The Divine Milieu*, Teilhard begins with the words of St. Paul: "No man lives or dies to himself. But whether through our life or through our death we belong to Christ."[24]   These words aptly express the heart of Teilhard's spirituality. For he was, indeed, like St. Paul, a missionary and an apostle who sought to bring about a fuller and plainer disclosure of God in the world. Teilhard himself would pray:

> And, I, Lord, for my (very lowly) part, would wish to be the apostle — and if I dare be so bold — the evangelist — *of your Christ in the universe* . . . . To bring Christ, by virtue of a specifically organic connexion, to the heart of realities that are esteemed to be the most dangerous, the most unspiritual, the most pagan — in that you have my gospel and my mission.[25]

1 See for example Robert Faricy, S.J., *The Spirituality of Teilhard de Chardin* (Minneapolis: Winston Press, 1981), p. 9. I found this book very helpful and I am very much indebted to it in this chapter.

2 Henri De Lubac writes: "We shall find that Père Teilhard gives us his spiritual doctrine by opening his soul to us." *The Religion of Teilhard de Chardin* (New York: Image Books, 1968), p. 21.

3 On this point Fr. Faricy notes: "This combination of sometimes clumsy gropings together with the expression of greatly important basic truths for today can be found reflected in church teaching. In 1962, the Holy Office in Rome issued a warning, which of course still has validity, that Teilhard's ideas might for various reasons lead Christians into error. And at the same time, the Second Vatican Council was preparing its most revolutionary and most important statement, *The Pastoral Constitution on the Church in the Modern World*, a statement that shows clearly its grounding in the fundamental orientation

and basic concepts of Teilhard's thought, which dominates the document."
Faricy, *op. cit.*, p. 12.

4 *The Making of a Mind: Letters from a Soldier-Priest, 1914-1919* (New York: Harper and Row, 1965); *Writings in Time of War* (New York: Harper and Row, 1959).

5 *The Divine Milieu* (New York: Harper and Row, 1960; Harper Torchbook edition published in 1965).

6 *The Phenomenon of Man* (New York: Harper and Row, 1959).

7 For an interesting treatment of the relationship of Teilhard to St. Paul, see the essay by Henri De Lubac, S.J., in *Teilhard Explained* (New York: Paulist, 1968), pp. 9-37.

8 Faricy, *op. cit.*, p. 44.

9 See Teilhard's "Cosmic Life" in *Writings in Time of War*, pp. 69-70.

10 Cited in Faricy, *op. cit.*, pp. 13-14.

11 Teilhard de Chardin, "My Universe" in *Science and Christ* (New York: Harper and Row, 1968), p. 65. See also *The Divine Milieu*, pp. 125-126.

12 Teilhard de Chardin "The Mass on the World" in *Hymn of the Universe* (New York: Harper and Row, 1965), p. 19.

13 For Teilhard the term 'Pleromization' means "the process of the progressive unification and reconciliation of all things in the risen Christ. He wants to find Jesus risen in all things precisely in that they are in process towards Christ-Omega." See Faricy, *op. cit.*, p. 45.

14 *The Divine Milieu*, p. 62.

15 *Ibid.*, p. 64.

16 *Ibid.*, p. 66.

17 Teilhard de Chardin, "Christology and Evolution" in *Christianity and Evolution* (New York: Harcourt, Brace, Jovanovich, 1971), p. 85.

18 See Teilhard's "Introduction to the Christian Life" in *Christianity and Evolution*, p. 163.

19 *The Divine Milieu*, p. 95 ff. See also his essay "Reflections on Happiness" in *Toward the Future* (New York: Harcourt, Brace, Jovanovich, 1975), pp. 117-120.

20 *The Divine Milieu*, pp. 96-97.

21 *Toward the Future*, p. 118.

22 Teilhard writes: "In other words: first, be. Secondly, love. Finally, worship." *Ibid.*, p. 120.

23 Faricy, *op. cit.*, pp. 83-84.

24 *The Divine Milieu*, p. 112.

25 See Teilhard's "The Priest" in *Writings in Time of War*, pp. 219-220.

# Caryll
# HOUSELANDER (1901-1954)

CARYLL HOUSELANDER died of cancer in London in 1954 at the age of 53. Much was accomplished during that relatively short life, for she was a remarkable and unique woman. She was a writer, an artist, a poet and a counselor to many suffering people who came to her seeking help. It is as a spiritual writer, however, that she is best known. Monsignor Ronald Knox was such an admirer of the spiritual writings of this English Catholic laywoman that he expressed the hope at one time that she would establish a school for the writers of spiritual books. He felt that "she seemed to see everything for the first time, and the driest of doctrinal considerations shone out like a restored picture when she had finished with it."[1]

Her basic message comes through clearly and forcefully in all her writings, namely that we must learn to see Christ in everyone. It is communion with Christ and communion with all others in Him that gives meaning to our lives. This message built upon her own experiences and developed over the years through her prayer and study. The insights gained through her own suffering and her contact with the suffering of those she counseled also played an important role. This added a sense of realism and practicality to her writings. She wrote with their experiences and problems in mind, and she sought to bring together the reality of Christ and the reality of the everyday experiences of the individual person. She wanted to present Christ's message as it affects us and has meaning in our daily lives.

Since her own experience plays such an important role in her writings, we will begin with her life and the significant events that shaped her spirituality. Secondly, we will consider the basic insights of her spirituality, Christ's indwelling presence in the individual, and the doctrine of the Mystical Body. Finally we will look at some of the practical applications she makes in the areas of prayer and human suffering.

# I

Caryll Houselander was baptized in the Catholic Church at the age of six. Influenced by an agnostic friend and a Catholic doctor, Caryll's mother decided that her two daughters should be brought up Catholic. Although Caryll was born into fairly comfortable surroundings, her early years were beset with many problems and difficulties. As a young girl she was frequently ill.

When she was around eight or nine she was attacked by a frightening illness that kept her bedridden for three months. This illness came upon her suddenly and, as she tells us in an autobiographical account, "made a deeper impression on my whole subsequent life than anything that ever happened to me before or since."[2]   Doctors were unable to diagnose the strange illness that was accompanied by great weakness, difficulty in breathing and a continual temperature. But this was nothing compared to the anguish of mind and spirit that was present. She was tormented with anxieties, feelings of guilt and scruples. Release from these torments and restored health came when she received Holy

Communion, given to her as Holy Viaticum, since she was thought to be close to death.

Caryll Houselander describes this event carefully for two reasons. First, it deepened profoundly her faith in Christ's presence in the Blessed Sacrament. Secondly, this childhood experience of anxiety neurosis conditioned her attitude toward psychological suffering. It left her acutely aware of such suffering in others and the suffering Christ in others. She writes: "It is largely my experience of these people and their suffering that has confirmed my faith in *Christ in Man*, which in a sense is what the Catholic Church is."[3] She ultimately would come to the conviction that it is only the "touch of God" that provides the real cure.

When Caryll was about nine years old, her stable home life came to an end with the separation of her parents. This proved to be very painful for her, and its traumatic effects would greatly influence her subsequent development. Any hopes for a secure home life were now ended and the following years would be spent at various boarding schools. Poor health in general and frequent bouts with serious sickness would also mark these years.

Although Caryll would later look back with fond memories of the French convent school she attended for a period, the years at the various boarding schools were not happy ones for her. She was singular and individualistic in many ways, and her shyness and introversion made it very difficult for her to relate to others. She tended to be critical and rebellious with a strong mind and will of her own.

Caryll's stay at an English convent school came to an abrupt end when she was sixteen. Her mother wanted her to return home to assist in what Caryll found to be a curious and puzzling situation. A priest friend of the family had left his religious order. Sick in mind and body and awaiting an assignment to a parish, he had taken refuge at the home of

Mrs. Houselander who now needed Caryll to assist her in caring for him. Although innocent in itself, it caused tongues to wag and Caryll found herself more or less ostracized by most of the Catholics she knew who took scandal at this arrangement. She also came to resent bitterly the lack of charity shown to the sick priest by his former Catholic friends.[4]

A year later Caryll won a scholarship to art school and began to move in different circles. She was now living on her own and barely supported herself with some work as a commercial artist. Her friends included Bohemians, artists and art students who for the most part were as poor as she was. Caryll found that many of them were as maladjusted to society in general as she had become, and thus she was more at ease with them than she had been with any other people.

During this period Caryll ceased being a practicing Catholic and began searching for some other form of Christianity. She went from one minister to another asking to be instructed in their beliefs, but nothing seemed to meet her deepest needs. During this period of searching and alienation from the Catholic Church she met and fell in love with Sidney Reilly, the famous international spy who later was shot by the Communists in Russia. Ultimately the relationship ended, either because her love was not fully reciprocated or because it was an ultimate hindrance in her return to the Church. But her love for him had been deep and one not easily forgotten.[5]

Caryll's time of searching and struggling gradually came to an end as she became more and more conscious that she was running away from the thing she really wanted — the Catholic Church. An experience that she had while travelling in an underground train, in which she sensed deeply Christ's presence in all men and women, played a strong part in her return. Its impact upon her was extraordinary and it proved to be the starting point for a renewed spiritual life that was to grow and develop throughout the years. She began to take very seriously her growth in faith, and the spiritual journal she began at this time attests to the seriousness, generosity and ordered discipline that marked her efforts to respond to God's grace working powerfully in her life.[6]

Caryll at this time also began to find regular employment as an artist in decorating churches, but gradually she came to devote more and more time to writing. It began through the influence of her Jesuit confessor who encouraged her to write and illustrate for *The Messenger of the Sacred Heart* and *The Children's Messenger*. Her contributions to these periodicals continued for many years.

Her first spiritual book emerged from the context of the Second World War that enveloped Europe and brought such suffering and tragedy to the lives of all in England. It was published in 1941 and entitled *This War is the Passion*. The work met with a very warm reception and greatly encouraged her in her hopes as a writer.

Her second book, *The Reed of God* (1944), met with even greater success and was to become the most widely read of all her books. It was to draw forth an immense amount of letters to Caryll from those who had read it. Over the years other books would follow such as *The Comforting of Christ*, *The Passion of the Infant Christ*, *The Risen Christ*, a fictional work, *The Dry Wood*, a book of poetry, *The Flowering Tree*, and the autobiographical account of her early years, *A Rocking-Horse Catholic*.

Writing for her was to become an important part of her life, not only a means of earning a livelihood but a vocation in which she found a real sense of communion with others. She once wrote to a friend: "I am certain that for me the real *Communio* with people is in writing, and this does not only apply to strangers but to my intimate friends; I have realized that when they keep me from writing they are actually destroying all hope of Communion between us."[7]

Next to her writing, Caryll's other major work involved her in counseling and helping a wide range of people in need. The well-known psychologist and neurologist, Dr. Eric Straus, began early in 1942 to ask her to see some of his young patients. From that time on, more and more mentally and emotionally disturbed people were sent to her by Dr. Straus and other doctors for help. Many were helped back to health and stability through her love, compassion and empathy. She seemed to have great insight into persons and an uncanny gift for reaching a wide range of distraught persons. She often spoke of herself as a neurotic and it seems that her own sufferings had helped to teach her the art of healing broken people. Her wide experience in this area and her own study and research led eventually to her important postwar book, *Guilt,* in which she developed extraordinary insights about the relation between the spiritual and the psychological.[8]

Mention should be made of the psychic gifts Caryll Houselander apparently possessed. It is usually referred to as extra sensory perception (ESP), the ability to gain knowledge beyond the normal ways of the five senses. Caryll never made much of this power and simply took it for granted. For her it was a natural gift and a help in her work but nothing more. Yet it certainly helped her in her understanding of other people and it was very much a part of her as a person.[9]

Caryll's life after the war thus settled into a pattern of writing and publishing, doing a little teaching, and spending long hours working with neurotics and talking with the many people who sought her out for help. Gradually health problems began to increase and finally she was diagnosed as suffering from cancer. The ensuing operation and a long stay in the hospital arrested the disease for a period and she continued her work as best she could. But the cancer returned and finally on October 12, 1954 Caryll Houselander slipped from time to eternity.

# *II*

It is clear from Caryll Houselander's published books and correspondence that the basis of the spiritual life for her was the indwelling presence of Jesus Christ in each of us.[10]  That we are *other Christs* through this indwelling was for her the foundation for everything else in the spiritual life. From this fundamental theme of the indwelling of Christ, she goes on to develop the broader theme of the Mystical Body of Christ. Toward the end of her life she would sum it up well with the words: "Thus in my own case the Blessed Sacrament and the indwelling presence of Christ in man give the meaning of life to me, and satisfy my most urgent need, which is for communion. Communion with Christ and in Him communion with all men."[11]

It was only toward the end of her life that Caryll shared in some autobiographical writings that earlier in her life she had experienced in a profound way the presence of Christ in others through what she referred to as three "visions." She makes it clear that in her case the experience came first and then theological understanding and development came with time — through her prayer, work, study and reflection. It will be helpful for us to look more closely at her account of these experiences that were so important for her and her spirituality.

*The Three "Visions"*

Caryll refers to these three incidents as "visions" for lack of another word. They were certainly a "seeing" for her, not with the eyes but with the mind. She speaks of them as a seeing of the mind in which the details were known very vividly as one sees a definite picture. She never made any claims that these incidents were supernatural experiences or visions. She readily admits that they were all capable of a variety of natural explanations. Whether they were really natural or supernatural experiences was not that important to her. What was very important for her was that "it was in this way that God began to show me the Passion of Christ in man, and no doubt He did so because it was only in this way that I could apprehend it."[12]

The first of the three experiences that made the doctrine of the indwelling presence of Christ in us such a reality for her took place while she was a young girl at the French convent school. Here all of the nuns were French with the exception of a young English woman and a Bavarian lay sister. The Bavarian sister knew little English and her French too was very limited, and so normal communication was very difficult for her. The outbreak of the First World War added to her sense of isolation and loneliness, given the strong anti-German sentiment present in England at the time.

One day Caryll passed what was referred to as the boot-room and saw the Bavarian sister sitting alone cleaning the children's shoes. She stopped and went in to offer to help her. Only when she drew closer did she see that the nun "was weeping soundlessly, tears pouring down her weather-beaten, rosy cheeks."[13]  Caryll stood there a long time, speechless with embarrassment, as children are by grown-ups' tears. She tells us: "At last I looked up and saw that the nun was wearing the Crown of Thorns. It was a great crown, more like a cap of thorns, covering her head, and so heavy that it bowed it down."[14]

Later, Caryll was to see that this experience was linked to the second "vision" she had in July, 1918. It occurred at the time she had drifted away from the Church, when, as she tells us, she "no longer recognized Christ, excepting in people who were poor or outcast or despised, and even in them my recognition was unrealistic."[15] One rainy evening she was on her way to a store when she stopped suddenly in the middle of a drab London street. There in front of her was what she could only call a gigantic and living Russian icon. It was an icon of Christ the King crucified:

> Christ was lifted above the world in our drab
> street, lifted up and filling the sky. His arms reach-
> ing, as it seemed, from one end of the world to the
> other, the wounds on His hands and feet rubies . . .
> Christ Himself, with His head bowed down by the
> crown, brooding over the world.[16]

Soon after this moving experience, perhaps the next day, she saw at the same street corner a placard announcing the assassination of the Tsar of Russia. She then understood more vividly the meaning of what she had seen previously, for the face of the Tsar in the newspaper photograph was the face of Christ the King in the icon without its glory. Although this "vision" was a brief one, it had a profound effect on her attitude to other people. It helped her to realize "that Christ is in kings as well as in outcasts, that His Passion in the world today is being lived out in kings as well as in common men."[17]

The third and most important "vision" for her came at the time she was seriously contemplating a definite break with the Catholic Church. This time the experience was on a much vaster scale than the other two and one that was more difficult to describe. It was not a seeing of Christ in one person, as was the case with the Bavarian nun, nor was it in one particular sort of person, as it had been in the living icon of Christ the King. This time it was Christ in all persons.

It occurred while she was traveling during the rush hour in a crowded underground train in London:

> I was in an underground train, a crowded train in which all sorts of people jostled together, sitting and strap-hanging — workers of every description going home at the end of the day. Quite suddenly I saw with my mind, but as vividly as a wonderful picture, Christ in them all. But I saw more than that; not only was Christ in every one of them, living in them, dying in them, rejoicing in them, sorrowing in them — but because He was in them, and because they were here, the whole world was here too, here in this underground train; not only the world as it was at that moment, not only the people in all the countries of the world, but all those people who had lived in the past, and all those yet to come.
>
> I came out into the street and walked for a long time in the crowds. It was the same here, on every side, in every passer-by, everywhere — Christ.[18]

This "vision" lasted with great intensity for several days, revealing the mystery and its implications for her more and more clearly. She came to see in a profound way the implications of the indwelling of Christ in every person. "Christ is one in all men, as He is One in countless Hosts; everyone is included in Him; there can be no outcasts, no excommunicates, excepting those who excommunicate themselves — and they too may be saved, Christ rising from death in them."[19]

After a few days, the "vision" faded. Christ was hidden once again for her, and in the years ahead she would see Christ in others only through an act of faith. But if the vision had gone from her, the knowledge remained, and she was to find that at the least touch of the Holy Spirit it was to flower again and again. For she saw that the knowledge gained from all three "visions" was like "a tiny little seed sown in the mind, which will increase and flower only through years of prayer and study of the doctrine of the Church, which invariably endorsed them."[20]

# III

Caryll Houselander's basic message built on these profound personal experiences and developed over the years through her own prayer and study. The theme of Christ in others became the dominant motif of her spirituality and appears over and over in her writings. It is to a fuller development of this theme that we now turn.

*Christ in Others*

For Caryll Houselander, this basic message can be put forth simply and clearly: "The core of happiness in every human relationship is our realization of the indwelling presence of Christ in one another."[21]   In a world that is confused by sin and suffering, it is only the love of Christ, Christ in us, that can make happiness possible amidst the varied relationships that are central to our lives. For it is only this love that can "sweeten all that is bitter, soften all that is hard, heal all that is wounded in our interrelated lives, infuse love where there was no love or even where there was antagonism, and moreover outlast life itself and flower in our immortality."[22]

Christ has given Himself to us and because of His presence in us we are all related to Him and to one another. We are all one with Him and through Him with one another. He has given Himself to us that we may give Him to one another. He comes to us in every person needing and asking for comfort, for sympathy, for understanding, for our friendship, and our love. He comes in the aged, the sick, the suffering.

To see Christ in others, of course, is not easy. It is particularly difficult in the case of those who are close to us, for always their human personality as we know it hides Him from us. There is only one way to overcome this difficulty. It is "simply by blind faith and the persevering practice, in our actions, of the contemplation of Christ in everyone, and in ourselves."[23]

The practice of contemplating Christ in others enables us to give Him the understanding, the compassion, the tenderness that He comes seeking in others. So often we are like the Samaritan Woman and do not know Him or recognize Him when He asks. Caryll Houselander expresses this poignantly when she writes:

> If we *knew* Who it is Who asks a million times for
> those simple, seemingly little human things that are
> the very essence of our relationship and which we
> can give through our every act, through the words
> we withhold or speak and the tone of voice in which
> we speak them, through the touch of our hands, the
> expression of our face! If only we knew![24]

Caryll recognizes that it is perhaps most difficult of all to realize Christ is in our lives. We may be so conscious of our sinfulness, our failures and our weaknesses that we are hesitant about acknowledging Christ's presence. She stresses, however, that it is immensely important to believe in Christ in ourselves because only then can we believe that He has given us the power and the potency of His love. Because of His gift, we are able to reach the whole world through those who are nearest at hand. Because Christ dwells in us, we are able to love "not merely with our own love, but with Christ's all powerful, all healing, all redeeming love."[25]

For Caryll there is one more vital point, and that is to realize that we can receive just as we can give. In fact receiving is a very great way of giving. We must keep in mind that we not only help to give an increase of the Christ-life to others through our human relations, but we also receive it from them. They too have the power of His love, and we depend upon them as much as they do upon us. "Just as our own shortcomings do not prevent us from giving Christ to others, theirs do not prevent them from giving Him to us."[26]

### The Role of Suffering

Along with this great faith in the presence of Christ within us and our oneness in Christ in His Mystical Body, Caryll Houselander was constantly aware of suffering in our lives. This was something she experienced profoundly in her own life and which she was acutely conscious of in the lives of others and the world at large. She would write simply: "Man's life in Christ is the life of the risen Christ, but it must be lived by men still taking up their Cross daily."[27]

The mystery of suffering for her was intimately connected with the mystery of sin in the world. Since sin still exists, suffering still exists. Suffering is the result of both original sin and actual sin. When Christ came into the world, He found suffering in the world. He did not obliterate suffering but he brought love and meaning to it. He did this by changing our suffering into His Passion, making it meaningful and fruitful. Through Him our suffering became redemptive. It has meaning because "all the suffering we see today, all the suffering we know in our own lives, is the passion of Christ. If Christ had not changed our suffering to His Passion, we should still have suffered, but suffering would have been futile, destructive and useless."[28]

Through Christ, then, suffering has become part of the mystery of salvation because Christ chose to suffer. It is not an evil to be avoided at all costs, but a thing to be accepted willingly, even joyfully, as a means to sharing in the redemption of the world.[29]  Because we are all one in Christ, because we are other Christs, His life and Passion continue in our life and suffering. Although our redemption was achieved completely by Christ, it does, by a special loving mercy of His, go on in us. It goes on continually in the Mystical Body of Christ, which we are.

At the end of her autobiographical account, Caryll has a passage that sums up much of her spirituality and the place of suffering in it:

> For me, the greatest joy in being once again in
> full union with the Catholic Church has been, and
> now is, the ever-growing reassurance given by
> the doctrine of the Mystical Body of Christ, with its
> teaching that we are the Church, and that "Christ
> and His Church are one" — and that because Christ
> and His Church are one, the world's sorrows, with
> which I have always been obsessed, and which is
> a common obsession in these tragic years, is only the

shadow cast by the spread arms of the Crucified
King to shelter us until the morning of the Resurrection from the blaze of everlasting love.[30]

# *IV*

These final remarks will focus on the role of prayer in
Caryll Houselander's writings. Although she does not treat
prayer in any systematic way it is certainly central to her
spirituality. It flows naturally from everything she wrote,
particularly her great emphasis on our union with Christ
and one another in His Mystical Body.

Prayer had a significant place in her life from the time
she returned to full communion in the Church as a young
woman. At that time of renewed fervor, she generously
sought to correspond to God's grace working powerfully in
her life. The journal she kept during these years attests to
this fervor and generosity, and to the importance she gave to
prayer in her daily life.[31]

As her strong sense of our union with one another in
Christ's Mystical Body developed, praying for others took
on great importance in her spiritual life. She would pray
particularly for those towards whom she felt some aversion
or bitterness. She found that it was prayer that could soften
her heart and allow her to see and love on a deeper level. In
fact she had a strong conviction that one really gets to know
people by praying for them.[32]

When Caryll wrote her first book, *This War is the Passion*,
during England's difficult days of World War II, she spoke
about "defenses of the mind" that would sustain a person
against the dehumanizing forces that were so prevalent at
the time. She stressed that prayer must be the first defense

for "prayer is a healing thing, and our first defense must begin to heal even while it fortifies us, and it must be the reserve on which we can draw over and over again."[33]    It is prayer that teaches us to concentrate, that leads us to absolute trust in God, and makes our minds ready for the essential things spoken of in the Gospels.

Since prayer for her must be woven into our daily lives, she was convinced that the habit of prayer must be maintained. We can pray all the time and everywhere; we can pray without ceasing as Christ urges us. If this does not come naturally, we must find ways that help us to learn.

Among the various ways, Caryll was fond of emphasizing the prayer of the body. We are not praying only when we are on our knees and saying a lot. For Caryll "you pray, when you pray well, with your body, with your hands and feet and head and heart, your ribs pray, your ears pray, your eyes pray."[34]    Our bodies — offered in sacrifice as the Host in the Mass is offered in sacrifice — are praying. If this is realized, then "every call on your energy, every ache in your limbs, even every yawn you stifle, will remind you of God."[35]

Another form of prayer that Caryll stresses was the prayer of relaxing in the Lord. Besides the prayer in which we offer ourselves to God, she felt there should be the prayer in which we let God give Himself to us. We should learn to receive and rest in the love of God in silence and joy:

> There should be, even in the busiest day, a few
> moments when we can close our eyes and let God
> possess us. He is always present, always giving us life,
> always round us and in us, like the air we breathe;
> there should be moments at least when we become
> more conscious of His presence; when we become
> conscious of it as the only reality, the only thing that
> will last for ever.[36]

*Rhythmic Prayer*

The notion of "rhythmic prayer" held a certain fascination for Caryll Houselander. With her poetic and creative temperament she sensed easily and profoundly the law of rhythm that is found in nature and the passing of time, as well as in our own bodies. It comes then as no surprise to her that the Church prays through just the same great rhythm passing from birth to death, from death to resurrection:

> The liturgical year is a year of Christ-rhythm, from His silence in the heart of Mary in Advent, gathering to His Passion, from His Passion to the darkness of the tomb, from the darkness of the tomb to the daybreak and "lumen Christi" of Easter morning. The Mass itself follows this very same rhythm exactly, and so does each day of the hours of the Office.[37]

From all this, she concludes "that rhythmic prayer must be pleasing to God, that He has designed us as He has designed everything else, to work by a rhythmical law, that we so really fulfill His will in us only when we are in harmony with His great rhythm."[38]

The habit of prayer initiates us into this movement. The rhythm of the Church's prayer goes on day after day, and members of the Church share in it because they are all one. But they increase the awareness of this when they deliberately join in the rhythmic prayer. This can be done by praying in many different ways — through the Eucharist, the Office, the Jesus Psalter, the rosary, etc. She would also suggest:

Perhaps the simplest way is always the closest
to Heaven, for the effect of rhythmic prayer is so to
quieten and ease the heart, that gradually prayer
does become just an intense consciousness of God
acting in us; we learn at last to realize that waking,
eating, loving and sleeping are the supreme prayers,
that we pray in so far as we concentrate our whole
selves, all our love, into God's will for us, and His will
is first of all that we live as human creatures, that we
rise and work and eat and love and sleep. Each day is
an image of our life, and if we come to pray with each
act of each day this rhythm will surely flow into our
life, which in the end we shall see simply as one cycle
of day and night.[39]

\*   \*   \*   \*   \*   \*   \*

The terms "ordinary" and "extraordinary" come to
mind when one reflects on the life of Caryll Houselander.
On the one hand, she was a talented, gifted and extraordinary woman. On the other hand, her life was characterized for the most part by doing ordinary, human things
with ordinary people. Yet she saw clearly and with great
insight the tremendous value and significance of all these
ordinary things when done in light of the Christ-life that
permeates us. It is through the ordinary that one can love
and serve God in an extraordinary way, and bring one's life
into harmony with God's providential love and will.

There is a very beautiful passage in her book, *The Risen
Christ*, which aptly illustrates her great belief in the significance of our lives, and her deep faith in the resurrection of
the dead. It summarizes, too, so much of her thought.

Everything falls away from us, even memories — even the weariness of self. This is the breaking of the bread, the supreme moment in the prayer of the body, the end of the liturgy of our mortal lives, when we are broken for and in the communion of Christ's love to the whole world.

But it is not the end of the prayer of the body. To that there is no end. Our dust pays homage to God, until the endless morning of resurrection wakens our body, glorified.[40]

---

1 Quoted by Masie Ward in her biography, *Caryll Houselander, The Divine Eccentric* (New York: Sheed and Ward, 1962), p. 3.

2 Caryll Houselander, *A Rocking-Horse Catholic* (New York: Sheed and Ward, 1955), p. 41.

3 *Ibid.*, pp. 49-50.

4 Cf. *A Rocking-Horse Catholic*, p. 100 ff. See also her account in *Born Catholics* (New York: Sheed and Ward, 1954), pp. 257-258.

5 For further details of their relationship, cf. Ward, *Divine Eccentric*, p. 67 ff. See also Robin Bruce Lockhart's *Ace of Spies* (New York: Stein and Day, 1968), p. 92 ff.

6 Cf. Ward, *Divine Eccentric*, "New Beginnings," p. 77 ff.

7 *Ibid.*, p. 198. She also writes: "The suggestion that I would be happier if I dropped my work for a bit is like telling me I would be healthier if I stopped breathing for a time! . . . My writing is both my life and my living, you know, quite literally and in that order." *Ibid.*, pp. 197-198.

8 Caryll Houselander, *Guilt* (New York: Sheed and Ward, 1951).

9 For a fuller treatment cf. Ward, *Divine Eccentric*, pp. 137-151.

10 I am indebted to the help received from the doctoral dissertation of Henry Murphy, S.J., *The Indwelling Presence of Christ in Man — The Basis of the Spiritual Theology of F. Caryll Houselander* (Catholic University of America, 1971).

11 *Born Catholics*, pp. 249-250.

12 *Ibid.*, p. 255.

13 *Ibid.*, p. 254.

14 *Ibid.*

15 *Ibid.*, p. 259.

16 *A Rocking-Horse Catholic*, p. 112.

17  *Born Catholics*, p. 260.

18  *A Rocking-Horse Catholic*, pp. 137-138.

19  *Ibid.*, p. 139.

20  *Born Catholics*, p. 261.

21  Caryll Houselander, "Christ In Men", *Integrity* (Sept., 1952), p. 2.

22  *Ibid.*, p. 3.

23  *Ibid.*, p. 6. She also writes: "We must learn to see Christ in others with the eyes of faith, because the whole orientation of our will, in which is the secret of peace, will depend whether we *act* as if we did see Christ in them or not." *The Risen Christ* (New York: Sheed and Ward, 1958), p. 32.

24  *Christ in Man*, p. 7.

25  *Ibid.*, p. 8. She also writes: "Thus in what we do to the nearest, to the person in our own home, or office, or shop, we reach out with the world-encompassing arm of the crucified Christ and embrace the whole world." *Ibid.*

26  *Ibid.*, p. 8.

27  *Guilt* (New York: Sheed and Ward, 1951), p. 82.

28  *This War is the Passion* (New York: Sheed and Ward, 1941), p. 157.

29  *Ibid.*, p. 159. She adds: "Sorrow has not ceased to be sorrow, but it is no longer simply a punishment, it is something with its power of healing in itself, something that redeems, something that makes joy possible to men." p. 173.

30  *A Rocking-Horse Catholic*, p. 113.

31  Cf. Ward, *Divine Eccentric*, p. 83.

32  *Ibid.*, p. 226.

33  *This War is the Passion*, p. 83.

34  *Ibid.*, p. 85.

35  *Ibid.*

36  *Ibid.*, p. 104. She also writes: "I ought to be able to relax, however, to stop being afraid, the moment I realize that I am in God's presence. I ought to want Him to make His love known to me; my prayer should just be accepting, trusting, and even in a sense, sleeping in that love." *Ibid.*, p. 106.

37  *Ibid.*, p. 110.

38  *Ibid.*, p. 111.

39  *Ibid.*, p. 114.

40  *The Risen Christ*, pp. 73-74.

# Dietrich
# BONHOEFFER (1906-1945)

THE LAST PICTURE that we have of Dietrich Bonhoeffer comes from the prison doctor who wrote many years later of Bonhoeffer's execution at the hands of the Nazis just before the end of the Second World War:

> On the morning of the day, some time between five and six o'clock, the prisoners were led out of their cells and the verdicts read to them. Through the half-open door of a room in one of the huts I saw Pastor Bonhoeffer still in his prison clothes, kneeling in fervent prayer to the Lord his God. The devotion and evident conviction of being heard that I saw in the prayer of this intensely captivating man, moved me to the depths.[1]

A little later, under the scaffold itself, Bonhoeffer knelt to pray for the last time. A few minutes later he was hanging from the scaffold, a victim of the Third Reich in its closing weeks. Three weeks later Hitler committed suicide and shortly after that the Third Reich in Germany fell from power.

Thus ended the life of Dietrich Bonhoeffer, Lutheran pastor, theologian, and patriot. The spirit of prayer that marked his last hours was something that had been much a part of his life. Throughout his full and active life which ended so prematurely at the age of 39, his intense faith in Christ and his spirit of prayer shone forth clearly and steadily. It is this aspect of his rich and varied life that we wish to focus upon in these pages. We will look at some aspects of his life that have a bearing on his own life of faith, secondly at some of the chief elements of his spirituality, and finally at some of his thoughts on prayer.

# *I*

At an early age Bonhoeffer decided to study theology and prepare for ordination as a Lutheran pastor. It was basically an independent decision on his part and one that was not marked at this time by any strong religious motivation or family influence. Christian ethical standards were deeply established in the Bonhoeffer family life, and elementary religious instruction had been given to the children. Bible reading and choral-singing were associated with the festivals of the Christian year, but there was virtually no church-going. As his friend and biographer Eberhard Bethge would later write:

> He was not yet impelled by any love of the church,
> by any organized, genuinely theological system of
> beliefs, or by a discovery of the Scriptures and their
> exegesis. His interest in the discipline of theology
> was still colored by an essentially worldly philosophy
> of life.[2]

Only later would Bonhoeffer discover the Church and the fuller dimensions of the Christian life.

Before beginning his theological studies in Berlin, Dietrich and his brother Klaus set out in the spring of 1924 on a three-month visit to Rome. This stay in Rome was to have a profound effect upon him for it added depth to his concept of the Christian life and led to his strong interest in the idea of the Church during his student years. As already noted, the concept of the Church and church-going itself had played little part in his life up to this point. "But now before his dazzled sight there blazed out the visible symbol of the Church Universal; the Church of Rome, the Church at the heart of the world. Without prejudice or anxiety, Bonhoeffer gave himself up to this new experience."[3] Holy Week found him attending various religious services in Rome and his journal reflects the strong impressions made upon him.

Upon returning from Rome, Bonhoeffer plunged into his academic studies at the University of Berlin, studying with such well-known theologians as Harnack, Seeberg, Holl, and Lietzmann. The most significant theological influence, however, came from the writings of Karl Barth who was teaching at this time at the University of Göttingen. Bonhoeffer completed his doctoral thesis in 1927 and after a year in which he served as a curate for the German community in Barcelona, he returned to Berlin to prepare his "Habilitation" thesis. A year at Union Theological Seminary in New York City rounded out his theological preparation, and in 1931 at the age of 25, Bonhoeffer became a lecturer in systematic theology at Berlin.

Bonhoeffer's promising academic career, however, was cut short by the political events occurring in Germany in the early 1930s. He set himself in opposition to the Nazis and it became clear where he stood in the evolving turmoil and division that took place in the German Church. It led to his decision to abandon his academic career when Hitler came to power in 1933, although he wasn't officially expelled from the university until 1936.

In his definitive study of Bonhoeffer, Bethge describes a movement taking place in his friend's life during 1931-1932 which he describes as the theologian becoming a Christian. Bonhoeffer himself would never call it a conversion but he recognized the significant changes that took place in his life at this time. It showed in his actions and it marked the beginning of a phase in his life which continued until 1939. Bonhoeffer now went regularly to church and he regularly engaged himself in systematic meditation on the Bible; he spoke of oral confession no longer merely theologically, but as an act to be carried out in practice; he talked more and more of a community life of obedience and prayer; and more and more frequently he quoted the Sermon on the Mount as a word to be acted upon.[4]

In a letter to a friend, Bonhoeffer himself describes some of these changes. He spoke of discovering the Bible in a new way and actually becoming a Christian. He admitted that he had prayed only very little up to that time, but he recognized that the Bible, and in particular the Sermon on the Mount, freed him from all that:

> Since then everything has changed. I have felt this plainly, and so have other people about me. It was a great liberation. It became clear to me that the life of a servant of Jesus Christ must belong to the Church, and step by step it became plainer to me how far that must go.[5]

One of Bonhoeffer's main responsibilities during the ensuing years involved him in the training of young pastors.

The struggles in the German Lutheran Church over Hitler's policies led to the formation of the Confessing Church and Bonhoeffer became one of its most active members. This Church gave him the commission to create and direct one of the handful of seminaries for the training of young pastors which they had set up. He became director of the seminary at Finkenwalde in Pomerania, and threw himself whole-heartedly into this important work. For all practical purposes it was an underground seminary and the work had to be carried out in a climate of persecution and uncertainty. But the work seemed to thrive and Bonhoeffer was instrumental in setting up a vibrant center of Christian living and learning.

His books, *The Cost of Discipleship* and *Life Together*, reflect the vision and spirit of his labors at the seminary. This work continued until it was closed by the Nazi authorities in September of 1937. The training of pastors continued under more restricted circumstances with the formation of collective pastorates, and Bonhoeffer continued the work under this form.

The late 1930s found Bonhoeffer moving into another distinct stage in his life. The political situation in Germany, of course, affected his life profoundly, particularly as the German war operation expanded more and more. There was a brief flight to the United States when Bonhoeffer feared that he was going to be called for military service. Although friends in America urged him to stay, he felt his place was in Germany and he returned after a couple of months. In a letter to Reinhold Niebuhr, Bonhoeffer wrote:

> I have made a mistake in coming to America. I must live through this difficult period of our national

> history with the Christian people of Germany. I will
> have no right to participate in the reconstruction
> of Christian life in Germany after the war if I do not
> share the trials of this time with my people.[6]

Bethge describes Bonhoeffer during this period of his life as the "contemporary man." At the beginning of 1939, Bonhoeffer the theologian and Christian was entering fully into his contemporary world. In spite of the risks involved he dedicated himself to political activity and he became involved in the conspiracy to overthrow Hitler. This was not an easy decision for him to make, for he knew it would cost him much. He felt he had to respond to a call that demanded a different sacrifice, the sacrifice even of a Christian reputation. He felt that this decision required him to give up even his inmost claim to righteousness and he assumed that he would not be able to return to the ministry once the facts of his activity came to light. For Bonhoeffer, however, his duty seemed clear, and with great bravery and heroism he gave himself to the dangerous course before him.

It led ultimately to his arrest by the Gestapo on April 5, 1943. Two long years of imprisonment were to stretch out before him. During the days of imprisonment Bonhoeffer kept to a daily routine of Bible reading, prayer, meditation and study. All hopes of liberation were shattered when another attempt to overthrow Hitler led to the execution of a number of political prisoners only weeks before the end of the war. Thus ended the life of this man of deep faith and heroic stature, but it was not the end of the legacy he was to leave behind.

# *II*

Let us turn now and look at some of the themes Bonhoeffer emphasized in his spiritual writings. Three themes stand out prominently: discipleship, Christian community, and involvement in the world.

Although the theme of discipleship had long engaged his prayerful attention, his interest was intensified during the time of his responsibility for the training of future pastors. His efforts led to the publication of *The Cost of Discipleship*, one of his most well-known books which has had much influence in both Protestant and Catholic circles. In this book Bonhoeffer develops his ideas on discipleship in conjunction with his exposition of the Sermon on the Mount. He seeks to show how Jesus calls us to be His disciples and what it means to follow Him. As he writes in the introduction:

> What did Jesus mean to say to us? What is his will for us today? How can he help us to be good Christians in the modern world? In the last resort, what we want to know is not, what this or that man, or this or that Church, have of us, but what Jesus Christ himself wants of us.[7]

Thus Christ is central to the notion of, and the call to, discipleship. We are summoned to follow Jesus not as a teacher or a pattern of the good life, but as the Christ, the Son of God. We are summoned to an exclusive attachment to His person. Discipleship without Jesus Christ is merely a way of our own choosing. "Christianity without the living Christ is inevitably Christianity without discipleship, and Christianity without discipleship is always Christianity without Christ."[8]

The call demands a complete response in faith and obedience. Bonhoeffer stresses that the disciple is face to face with a reality that makes absolute demands — the reality of Christ. Certain definite steps must take place when one follows Christ. For Bonhoeffer, "the first step, which follows the call, cuts the disciple off from his previous existence. The call to follow at once produces a new situation. To stay in the old situation makes discipleship impossible."[9]

In Bonhoeffer's mind, discipleship is intimately connected with the Cross. Jesus makes it clear that suffering applies to His disciples no less than to Himself. The cross is laid on every Christian and the first Christian suffering which everyone must experience is the call to abandon the attachments of the world. "When Christ calls a man, he bids him come and die . . . but it is the same death every time — death in Jesus Christ, the death of the old man at his call."[10]    Thus for Bonhoeffer, suffering is the badge of true discipleship. And yet it is still a spirit of joy that marks the response:

> And if we answer the call to discipleship, where will it lead us? What decisions and partings will it demand? To answer this question we shall have to go to him; for only he knows the answer. Only Jesus Christ who bids us follow him, knows the journey's end. But we do know that it will be a road of boundless mercy. Discipleship means joy.[11]

Bonhoeffer likewise stresses that through the call of Christ we become individuals in the sense that Christ delivers us from immediacy with the world and brings us into immediacy with Himself. And in that immediacy with Him we are united to all other persons and things, for "*He is the*

*Mediator*, not only between God and man, but between man and man, between man and reality."[12]

What, then, is the nature of this life by which we are united to all things through Christ? What does it mean to be a Christian? Bonhoeffer summarizes this very forcefully:

> What does it really mean to be a Christian? Here we meet the word which controls the whole chapter, and sums up all we have heard so far. What makes the Christian different from other men is the "*peculiar*," the *perisson*, the "extraordinary," the "unusual," that which is not "a matter of course.". . . . What is the precise nature of the *perisson*? It is the life described in the beatitudes, the life of the followers of Jesus, the light which lights the world, the city set on the hill, the way to self-renunciation, of utter love, of absolute purity, truthfulness and meekness. It is unreserved love for our enemies, for the unloving and the unloved, love for our religious, political and personal adversaries. In every case it is the love which was fulfilled in the cross of Christ. What is the *perisson*? It is the love of Jesus Christ himself, who went patiently and obediently to the cross — it is in fact the cross itself. The cross is the differential of the Christian religion, the power which enables the Christian to transcend the world and to win the victory. The *passio* in the love of the Crucified is the supreme expression of the "extraordinary" quality of the Christian life.[13]

We are called to love, then, with an unconditional gift of our lives to other people. The disciples of Christ are to love unconditionally. Such love as this, of course, can only be the fruit of grace, that grace which must be sought and which costs us everything:

> Costly grace is the gospel which must be *sought* again and again, the gift of which must be *asked* for, the door at which a man must *knock*. Such grace is *costly* because it costs a man his life, and it is grace because it gives a man the only true life.[14]

### Christian Community

A second major theme in Bonhoeffer's spirituality is that of Christian community. This is developed in his *Life Together*, a book which flowed from the lived-out situation of the underground seminary at Finkenwalde. In developing his thoughts on community, he stresses first that the visible Christian community is a grace — a gift of God that should not be taken for granted. Those who have the privilege of living a common Christian life must be ready to declare gratefully that "it is grace, nothing but grace, that we are allowed to live in community with Christian brethren."[15]

Secondly, Bonhoeffer stresses that it is Christ who is at the center of every Christian community. We belong to one another through and in Jesus Christ for He alone is our unity. "Through him alone do we have access to one another, joy in one another, and fellowship with another."[16]   Since Christian community is founded solely on Jesus Christ, it is a spiritual and not a psychic reality. For Bonhoeffer the basis of all spiritual reality is the clear manifest Word of God in Jesus Christ. In the community of the Spirit the Word of God alone rules.

Bonhoeffer also writes about community with a realistic outlook that obviously flowed from his actual community life with the seminarians. He realizes that if Christian community springs from a wish dream or any preconceived notion of what it should be, it easily breaks down. It is not an ideal that we must realize but rather a reality created by God in Christ in which we may participate. Thus we should enter a Christian community not as demanding persons but as thankful recipients for the many blessings received. Bonhoeffer stresses that "in the Christian community thankfulness is just what is anywhere else in the Christian life. Only he who gives thanks for little things receives the big things."[17]

In *Life Together*, Bonhoeffer is particularly interested in developing the ways that a community is strengthened and nourished in its purpose. Among the many aspects of the day together, corporate prayer of the members assumes great importance. In Bonhoeffer's mind, the morning does not belong to the individual but to the Church of the triune God, to the Christian family, to the brotherhood. Thus, common life under the Word begins with common worship. The community gathers to praise God at the beginning of each day.

Although there will be differences for various groups, Bonhoeffer feels that the corporate prayer in the morning should include three elements: the reading of Scripture, the singing of the hymns of the Church, and the prayer of the fellowship.

He advocates the continuous or consecutive reading from Scripture — a chapter from the Old Testament and at least a half of a chapter of the New Testament each morning. Great stress is also placed on the Book of Psalms since he recognizes the Psalter as the great school of prayer.

Singing should be an integral part of the common worship for we are constantly urged in the Psalter to "Sing unto the Lord a new song." It should involve singing from the heart, singing to the Lord, singing the Word, singing in unity.

The prayer of the fellowship concludes the common worship and "this prayer must really be our word, our prayer for this day, for our work, for our fellowship, for the particular needs and sins that oppress us in common, for the persons who are committed to our care."[18]

Bonhoeffer would have the community come together also at the close of the day to pray again in common. Once more there should be the reading from Scripture, the prayer of the Psalms, a hymn and common prayer. The evening is an appropriate time for common intercession.

After stressing the importance of the community coming together to pray, to work, and to recreate, Bonhoeffer goes on to emphasize the importance of periods of solitude and silence. As he puts it so well: "Let him who cannot be alone beware of community" and "Let him who is not in community beware of being alone."[19]   The day also needs definite times of silence, silence under the Word and silence that comes out of the Word. According to Bonhoeffer, there are three purposes for which the Christian needs a definite time to be alone during the day: Scripture meditation, prayer, and intercession. All three should have their place in the daily period of meditation.

Two other points might be mentioned briefly in connection with Bonhoeffer's treatment of community.

First he focuses attention on the necessity of ministry or service within the community. He speaks of the ministry of holding one's tongue, the ministry of meekness, the ministry of listening, the ministry of helpfulness, the ministry of bearing, the ministry of proclaiming, and the ministry of authority.

Secondly, he develops some interesting connections between the practice of confession and the building up of community. In confession the breakthrough to community takes place, for sin isolates a person and withdraws him from the community. Sin wants to remain alone, it shuns the light. But it is in confession that "the light of the Gospel breaks into the darkness and seclusion of the heart."[20]

*Christian Involvement*

Another major theme of Bonhoeffer's spirituality is that of the Christian's involvement in, and identification with, the world. This was foremost in Bonhoeffer's religious thoughts since his early days as a minister. For example, in one of the sermons he preached during his year in Barcelona just before his ordination, there is the reminder that the Christian must not forsake the world. He urged his listeners: "If you want to find God, be faithful to the world."[21]

Bonhoeffer's interest in this issue intensified as his own political involvement increased in the year 1939. He made the decision to involve himself deeply in the politics of Germany and the conspiracy to overthrow Hitler. He made the decision knowing full well the dangers involved and the cost to him personally and religiously. Yet he felt that this was where God was leading him and that his duty lay in this direction.

During his long confinement in prison, one of Bonhoeffer's projects was to attempt to reshape his theology and to grapple with the role of the Christian in the modern world. The basic ideas of this quest are contained in the letters he sent to his friend, Eberhard Bethge, who later published them as the *Letters and Papers from Prison.*

Bonhoeffer struggled with such questions as how to claim for Jesus Christ a world that has come of age, and the nonreligious interpretation of Biblical terms in such a world. These investigations were carried out in a spirit of prayer. He writes at the outset of these studies: "But even if we are prevented from clarifying our minds by talking things over, we can still pray, and it is only in the spirit of prayer that any such work can be begun and carried through."[22]

In a forceful letter of July 21, 1944, he writes on this subject:

> Later I discovered and am still discovering up to this very moment that it is only by living completely in this world that one learns to believe. One must abandon every attempt to make something of one-self, whether it be a saint, a converted sinner, a churchman (the priestly type, so called!), a righteous man or an unrighteous one, a sick man or a healthy one. This is what I mean by worldliness — taking life in one's stride, with all its duties and problems, its successes and failures, its experiences and helpless-ness. It is in such a life that we throw ourselves utterly in the arms of God and participate in his sufferings in the world and watch with Christ in Gethsemane. That is faith, that is *metanoia*, and that is what makes a man and a Christian.[23]

There has been a tendency on the part of some since the appearance of the *Letters* to oversimplify Bonhoeffer's thought and to take his fragmentary remarks in his letters apart from the total thrust of his life and writings. Bethge is careful to avoid this, and he is at pains to integrate the letters with the fullness of Bonhoeffer's thought. He stresses in particular the importance of the "arcane discipline" for Bonhoeffer.[24]   Basically, the term refers to the many as-pects that make up the Christian identity. For Bonhoeffer the task for the Church was to be fully identified with the modern world without losing her identity. This is really the question of the relationship between prayer and action and the tension that can easily arise. One interpreter of Bonhoeffer's thought, following Bethge, writes on this question:

> For him, as for Bethge, the means by which identity was to be maintained was defined by the phrase "secret discipline", while the demands of identification were summed up in the term "religionless Christianity", or more often "non-religious interpretation of the Gospel". Secret discipline meant for him all that had power to deepen and sustain Christian life: prayer, meditation, common worship, the sacraments, and experiments in life together such as Finkenwalde had been, all in fact that helped to fit the Christian for a life of love lived with God and for his fellow men. It meant besides a recognition of the fact that the truths of the gospel can and must be shared with fellow Christians in a way different from that by which they may be communicated to others, while religionless Christianity meant the Christian's openness to those others, it meant his complete and joyful openness to the whole multifarious world around him, it meant his being without any reserve the man for others.[25]

Bonhoeffer's life represents a continuous effort to hold these two aspects of the Christian life in balance. External events in his life caused him to emphasize one of these at particular times and in certain circumstances. For example, the subject of Christian identity came to the fore during the years of his seminary work and flowered in *The Cost of*

*Discipleship* and *Life Together*. During his last few years he was preoccupied with the practical and theological problems of identification with the world, and the *Letters* show the direction his thought was taking. We can only speculate how his attempts to integrate and balance both aspects would have continued, but we can be sure on the basis of Bonhoeffer's deep faith and the witness of his life that the exploration of the means of identification with the world would never have been pursued at the price of his Christian identity.

# III

Although it has never really been absent from our discussion so far, we can focus more directly now on the place prayer played in Bonhoeffer's own life and some of his specific thoughts on the subject of prayer. Bonhoeffer doesn't write about prayer in any systematic way but its importance for him emerges very clearly, particularly in his own daily life as a Christian.

Bonhoeffer seemed to approach everything he did with a certain seriousness and intensity. Once he became convinced of the importance of something, he gave himself to it in a disciplined and energetic way. This attitude seemed to characterize his approach to prayer. He was convinced that one has to work at one's life of prayer, giving it time and attention. In one of his early sermons he reflects this orientation as he urges:

> Our relationship with God must be practised, otherwise we shall not find the right note, the right word, the right language when he comes upon us unawares. We have to learn the language of God,

learn it with effort, we must work at it, if we too
would learn to converse with Him; prayer too must
be practised as part of our work.[26]

As noted earlier, regular scriptural meditation had become a part of Bonhoeffer's daily order since, as he tells us,
he had discovered the Bible in a new way and had actually
become a Christian. His systematic meditation on the
Sermon on the Mount in particular had been a very freeing
experience for him, and from the time of that awakening, he
was convinced of the importance of regular prayer and
scriptural meditation.

It is not surprising, then, that Bonhoeffer made prayer,
both corporate and private, an integral part of the order of
the day in the seminary at Finkenwalde. He was at pains to
introduce the practice of meditation to the seminarians
since for practically all of them this was a new type of
experience of prayer. Bonhoeffer's own personal example
was no doubt as effective as his teaching and training.

Bonhoeffer always found in prayer a source of strength
and unity. For example, he realized that the young pastors
would face many obstacles and discouragements after they
left Finkenwalde and began their service in the Confessing
Church. Each month a circular letter went out from the
House of Brothers at Finkenwalde assuring these men of
the steady support of their old seminary and the reality of
their communion through prayer. One such letter urged
them:

> Dear Brothers, in times such as those that lie ahead
> of us we cannot arm ourselves otherwise than by
> strong and persistent prayer, and now we shall see
> whether our life and prayer have really been a pre-
> paration for this hour when we must confess our

faith. If we persevere in prayer, then we can have confidence that the Holy Spirit will give us the right words at the time when we need them, and that we shall be found faithful.[27]

During his own extended period in prison, Bonhoeffer's regular prayer was a main source of his courage and equanimity. From his first days of imprisonment, he set up for himself a strict regime from which he did not depart. This included various exercises of prayer: meditation, intercession, thanksgiving, praying the Psalms, and Bible study. We know, too, that for the Christmas of 1943 he wrote prayers for the other prisoners. These prayers flowed from his own prayer, the daily use of the Psalter and the hymns he knew so well. It should be noted, too, that Bonhoeffer counted on the prayers of his friends while he was in prison. For example, in the last letter Bethge received from him, Bonhoeffer wrote:

> Please don't ever get anxious or worried about
> me, but don't forget to pray for me — I'm sure you
> don't! I am so sure of God's guiding hand that I hope
> I shall always be kept in that certainty. You must
> never doubt that I am travelling with gratitude and
> cheerfulness along the road where I am being led.[28]

Let us look a little more closely now at meditation since, as we have seen, it was something Bonhoeffer practiced faithfully in his own life and taught carefully to the seminarians at Finkenwalde. He develops many of his own reflections on the subject in his book *Life Together* where he strongly advocates a regular period of meditation each day:

There are three purposes for which the Christian
needs a definite time when he can be alone during
the day: Scripture meditation, prayer, and intercession. All three should have their place in the daily
period of meditation.[29]

For Bonhoeffer the time of meditation allows us essentially to be alone with the Word; we wait for God's Word to
address us personally. This is why we begin our meditation
with the prayer that God may send His Holy Spirit to us
through His Word and reveal His Word to us and enlighten
us. In meditation we confine ourselves to a brief selected
text of Scripture which possibly we may keep for a whole
week, for meditation seeks to go into "the unfathomable
depths of a particular sentence and word." As Bonhoeffer
writes:

In our meditation we ponder the chosen text on
the strength of the promise that it has something
utterly personal to say to us for this day and for our
Christian life, that it is not only God's Word for
the Church, but also God's Word for us individually.
We expose ourselves to the specific word until it
addresses us personally. And when we do this, we are
doing no more than the simplest, untutored Christian does every day; we read God's Word as God's
Word for us.[30]

Bonhoeffer lists some practical points and applications.
First, it is not necessary that we should get through the
entire scriptural passage in one meditation. If a person is
moved and arrested by one sentence or even one word,
there is no need to move on. Nor is it necessary that we be
concerned in our meditation to express our thought and

prayer in words. Unphrased thought and prayer may often be more beneficial. There is also no need to discover new ideas in meditation. It is sufficient if the Word, as we read and understand it, penetrates and dwells within us. It will do its work in us, often without our being conscious of it.[31]

Bonhoeffer also stresses that there is no need to have an unexpected extraordinary experience in meditation. This can happen, of course, but if it does not, it is not a sign that the meditation period had been unprofitable. We must expect times of spiritual dryness, apathy, aversion, and even inability to pray. We must center our attention not on ourselves but on the Word alone. The fundamental rule of all meditation for Bonhoeffer is to seek God alone, not happiness. "If you seek God alone, you will gain happiness: that is its promise."[32]

Ultimately, it is to personal prayer that meditation should lead:

> The Scripture meditation leads to prayer. We have already said that the most promising method of prayer is to allow oneself to be guided by the word of the Scripture, to pray on the basis of a word of Scripture. In this way we shall not become the victim of our own emptiness. Prayer means nothing else but the readiness and willingness to receive and appropriate the Word, and what is more, to accept it in one's personal situation, particular tasks, decisions, sins and temptations. . . . According to a word of Scripture we pray for the clarification of our day, for preservation from sin, for growth and sanctification, for faithfulness and strength in our work. And we may be certain that our prayer will be heard, because it is a response to God's Word and promise. Because

God's Word has found its fulfillment in Jesus Christ,
all prayers that we pray conforming to this Word are
certainly heard and answered in Jesus Christ.[33]

What is the test of meditation? For Bonhoeffer it is
found in the time away from prayer and in the actions of the
day itself. This is where we find whether the Christian's
meditation has led into the unreal, or whether it has led into
a real contact with God, from which a person emerges
strengthened and purified. The main test of prayer for
Bonhoeffer is:

> Has it transported him for a moment into a spiritual
> ecstasy that vanishes when everyday life returns, or
> has it lodged the Word of God so securely and
> deeply in his heart that it holds and fortifies him,
> impelling him to active love, to obedience, to good
> works? Only the day can decide.[34]

The prayer of intercession also plays an important part
in Bonhoeffer's thinking on prayer, particularly in the context of community life. In his mind, a Christian fellowship
collapses if it does not live and exist by the intercession of its
members for one another. Christians who begin to pray for
others make the happy discovery that they can no longer
condemn or hate someone for whom they pray. This is
because intercession means to bring another into the
presence of God, to see that person under the Cross of Jesus
as a poor human being and sinner in need of grace. "To
make intercession means to grant our brother the same
right that we have received, namely to stand before Christ
and share in his mercy."[35]

Finally, we might briefly note Bonhoeffer's reflections
on the relationship between self-denial and prayer. He

recognizes that it is hard to pray with cheerfulness or to devote oneself to a life of service which calls for much self-renunciation when the flesh is satisfied. Therefore, as Bonhoeffer writes in *The Cost of Discipleship*:

> We have to practise strictest daily discipline; only so can the flesh learn the painful lesson that it has no rights of its own. Regular daily prayer is a great help here, and so is daily meditation on the Word of God, and every kind of bodily discipline and asceticism.[36]

\* \* \* \* \* \* \*

Dietrich Bonhoeffer in his life and death stands out as a witness of faith. He was a brilliant, active, and intense person who was greatly influenced by the events that swirled around him in a critical period of German history. His active years as a pastor and theologian were lived out in a context of persecution, controversy and danger. One does not have to agree with all his decisions and reflections to recognize his steadfast love of Jesus Christ and his perseverance in his faith. He is an example of a dedicated Christian who lived intensely and wholeheartedly. Through the example of his own life, he inspired others to generosity, steadfastness and heroic sacrifice. In his writings he spoke out in a forceful and challenging way. The legacy of both will live. Part of that legacy might be summed up in the words a fellow prisoner later wrote of him: "He was one of the very few men I have ever met to whom his God was real, and ever close to him."[37]

---

1  Mary Bosanquet, *The Life and Death of Dietrich Bonhoeffer* (New York: Harper and Row, 1968), p. 15.

2 Eberhard Bethge, *Dietrich Bonhoeffer, Man of Vision, Man of Courage* (New York: Harper and Row, 1970), p. 29.
3 Bosanquet, p. 52.
4 Bethge, p. 154.
5 *Ibid.*, pp. 154-155.
6 *Ibid.*, p. 559.
7 Dietrich Bonhoeffer, *The Cost of Discipleship* (New York: Macmillan, 1963), p. 37.
8 *Ibid.*, pp. 63-64.
9 *Ibid.*, p. 66.
10 *Ibid.*, p. 99.
11 *Ibid.*, p. 41.
12 *Ibid.*, p. 106.
13 *Ibid.*, pp. 169-170.
14 *Ibid.*, p. 47.
15 Dietrich Bonhoeffer, *Life Together* (New York: Harper and Row, 1954), p. 20.
16 *Ibid.*, p. 39.
17 *Ibid.*, p. 29.
18 *Ibid.*, p. 62.
19 *Ibid.*, p. 77.
20 *Ibid.*, p. 112.
21 Bosanquet, p. 72.
22 Bethge, p. 757.
23 Dietrich Bonhoeffer, *Letters and Papers from Prison.* Edited by Eberhard Bethge. (New York: Macmillan, 1962), pp. 226-227.
24 Bethge, p. 784 ff.
25 Bosanquet, p. 279.
26 *Ibid.*, p. 70.
27 *Ibid.*, p. 170.
28 *Ibid.*, p. 264.
29 *Life Together*, p. 81.
30 *Ibid.*, p. 82.
31 *Ibid.*, p. 83.
32 *Ibid.*, p. 84.
33 *Ibid.*, pp. 84-85.
34 *Ibid.*, p. 88.
35 *Ibid.*, p. 86.
36 *The Cost of Discipleship*, p. 189.
37 Bosanquet, p. 272.

# Columba
# MARMION (1858-1923)

THE SPIRITUAL AND THEOLOGICAL WRITINGS which flow from the Benedictine tradition have had a richly deserved position of prominence in the history of spirituality. Columba Marmion, the Irish-born priest who joined the Benedictines at Maredsous in Belgium and who later became its abbot, is an illustrious twentieth century example of that rich tradition.

Marmion's main writings, *Christ the Life of the Soul, Christ in His Mysteries*, and *Christ the Ideal of the Monk*, were based on the monastic and retreat conferences he gave over the years. As the titles indicate, they are centered on the person of Christ and they comprise Marmion's synthesis of the spiritual life.

His writings met with widespread acceptance and soon brought to the author a reputation as one of the foremost spiritual masters of the twentieth century. This was due to a number of reasons. First, his writings were firmly rooted in Scripture and doctrine. Secondly, it was recognized that he had a particular gift for explaining profound truths of the Christian faith with great simplicity and directness. Thirdly, there is a spirit of prayer that penetrates all of his spiritual conferences and writings. His clear purpose in all his writings was to direct the eyes and hearts of the reader to Jesus Christ and His Word.

In our development of Marmion's spiritual doctrines, we will focus first on his life and the main characteristics of his spirituality. Secondly, there will be a development of the themes that are prominent in his synthesis of the spiritual life. Finally, his reflections on the importance and nature of prayer will be considered.

# *I*

Joseph Marmion was born in Dublin, Ireland, on April 1, 1858, the son of an Irish father and a French mother. After graduating from Belvedere College in 1874 he entered Holy Cross Seminary at Clonliffe, just outside of Dublin. He studied philosophy there and then began his theological studies in preparation for ordination as a diocesan priest. He completed his study of theology at the Irish College and the College of the Propaganda in Rome and was ordained there on June 16, 1881. Returning to Ireland, he worked for a year as a parish priest and then returned to the seminary at Clonliffe to teach philosophy.

The roots of his attraction to the Benedictine way of life go back to his student days in Rome and to a visit to the famed abbey of Monte Casino. On his way back to Ireland from Rome as a young priest, he stopped off at the Abbey of Maredsous in Belgium to visit a priest friend. Five years later, as a young priest of 28, he would leave Ireland and his work at the seminary and return to Maredsous as a Benedictine novice.

Marmion's life as a Benedictine can be conveniently divided into three distinct periods, each of a duration of roughly ten years.

The first, extending from his entrance in 1886 until 1899, was spent at the abbey of Maredsous, first undergoing his own monastic formation and then serving as assistant to the master of novices.

The second period, extending from 1899 to 1909, was spent at the abbey of Mont-César at Louvain. Here Marmion taught dogmatic theology to the young monks and served as prior of the abbey. His long friendship with Cardinal Mercier, who was then the president of the Seminaire Leon XIII, goes back to this period at Louvain in Belgium.

The third period was marked by his return to Maredsous as abbot. He was elected abbot in 1909 and remained in this position until his death in 1923. The First World War took place during these years, making it a difficult time for the abbey and its leader, since Belgium was under German occupation for the duration of the war.

From the time of his solemn profession as a Benedictine, Dom Marmion was engaged in steady apostolic work. Invitations to preach soon came his way and these invitations increased as the years went by. He gave spiritual conferences to his fellow monks and other religious and gradually became very well known as a retreat director. To the extent that his other work allowed, he accepted invitations to give retreats to seminarians, diocesan priests, and religious men and women of various congregations. Throughout these years, he served as confessor and spiritual director to a large number of people. Thus his pastoral work and influence extended far beyond the limits of his monastery. His written works were based on his spiritual and retreat conferences, and their widespread publication greatly increased the scope of his influence.

The written works of Marmion had an interesting and somewhat unusual origin.[1] It was soon recognized at Maredsous that his conferences were of such a quality that they deserved to be recorded and published. Marmion himself had neither the time nor the inclination to do this himself. The actual writing was the work of one of the monks at Maredsous who knew his thought and style very well. He had at his disposal a considerable collection of notes of the conferences given by Marmion, some taken down in shorthand, others carefully noted by the attentive listeners. The editor compiled these notes seeking to reproduce the original conferences as closely as possible. The text was then given to Marmion to read over and to make any corrections or emendations.

In this way his famous trilogy was published: *Christ the Life of the Soul* (1918), *Christ in His Mysteries* (1919), and *Christ the Ideal of the Monk* (1922). These works met with widespread acceptance and acclaim as spiritual classics; they were translated into several languages and went through many editions. To this basic trilogy we can add his smaller work *Sponsa Verbi* (1923), and the popular *Christ the Ideal of the Priest* (1951), published long after his death but based on original manuscripts.

*Characteristics of Marmion's Spirituality*

Since the genesis of all Marmion's writings is found in the spiritual conferences that he gave, there is a distinct purpose and way of approach present in all his books. On Marmion's part they are the fruit of reflection and prayer more than study. He states his intent very clearly in *Christ the Life of the Soul* where he writes: "My object in these, as in all instructions, is to fix the eyes and the hearts of my readers on Jesus Christ and His word. He is the Alpha and the Omega of all sanctity and His word is the divine seed, from which sanctity springs."[2]   He felt convinced that if he could deliver God's message in God's own words, according to the divine simplicity of His plan, the message itself would produce wonders of sanctity.

His purpose, then, was to remind his readers of God's love and goodness as shown in the divine plan of our adoption in Jesus Christ. His explicit starting point would be the text of St. Paul at the beginning of the Letter to the Ephesians that God chose us in Christ "before the foundation of the world that we should be holy and unspotted in His sight in charity. Who hath predestinated us unto the adoption of children through Jesus Christ unto Himself, according to the purpose of His Will."[3]  Thus, Marmion seeks to lead us from an awareness and realization of the Divine Plan to the actual living it out in our lives, that is, to live out what we are, adopted children of God in Christ Jesus.

*Doctrinal Content*

A special characteristic of all Marmion's spiritual conferences is his strong doctrinal content. His particular training and background help us to understand this doctrinal foundation. As a student in Rome, he studied dogmatic theology under the renowned theologian Satolli, who exercised a very positive influence upon the young seminarian and student of theology.[4]   Later his many years as a professor of theology in the Benedictine abbey of Mont-César enabled him to develop and deepen his grasp of Catholic theological doctrine. During his years of teaching, he made a special study of the writings of St. Thomas Aquinas and this influence is apparent in all his writings.

It is important to keep in mind, however, that for Marmion the theological doctrine he develops is not an end in itself. Theology is not present in his writings for its own sake nor for any apologetic purpose, but because of its bearing on the spiritual life. He sought to present a synthesis of Christian dogmas in their relation to the spiritual life. Thus there is an intimate connection between theology and spirituality in the writings of Columba Marmion. His spirituality flowed from his theology and his theology was used for his exposition of the spiritual life.

With Marmion, then, we have an integrating of theology and spirituality that is somewhat rare. As the history of theology attests, often both theology and spirituality have gone their separate ways with negative results for both. Marmion is careful to present solid theology and solid spirituality. This provides one of the strongest points in his spiritual writings and it is one of the main reasons they have met with such widespread acceptance.[5]

A second major characterisic of Columba Marmion's spiritual writing is his strong emphasis on Scripture, with many references to the Gospels and the writings of St. Paul. This should come as no surprise as we recall the important place that a prayerful reading of Scripture plays in the Benedictine tradition. Marmion's own monastic and spiritual life was nourished continually by the prayerful reading of Scripture.

St. Paul was a particular favorite, and his influence clearly shows itself in all Marmion's spiritual conferences. He had a deep and intuitive grasp of the teaching of St. Paul that flowed from his own prayerful reading of the Pauline epistles. In Marmion's contemplation of Christ and the mystery of redemption, St. Paul is an important guide. In *Christ the Life of the Soul*, he begins with the opening passage in the Epistle to the Ephesians and takes this as his basis for unfolding God's plan of redemption and the sanctification of human persons.

St. Paul's influence is very strong, too, in *Christ in His Mysteries*. For Marmion, all the teaching of St. Paul is summed up in the knowledge of Christ.[6]   It is this knowledge that is the true basis of piety and a source of joy. For Marmion, "this knowledge acquired by faith, in prayer, under the inspiration of the Holy Spirit, is truly the foundation of living water springing up unto everlasting life."[7]

It should be noted, too, that Marmion's thought owes much to the Fourth Gospel. In stressing Christ's role as our only mediator, he derives much from Christ's Farewell Discourse (John, chs. 14-17).

The third important characteristic that is evident in Marmion's writings is the Benedictine influence. We have seen that he integrated very well his theology and his spirituality. This was due in no small measure to his Benedictine heritage that has a rich tradition of the love of learning and the pursuit of holiness. It has been noted, too, that Marmion's knowledge and love of Scripture flowed very naturally from his Benedictine monastic vocation with its tradition of "lectio divina", the prayerful reading of Scripture as prescribed in St. Benedict's rule. Then, too, the rhythm of the Church's liturgical celebration that is so much a part of Benedictine monastic life plays its part. In fact it would seem that his book *Christ in His Mysteries* owes much to the influence upon him of the repeated contemplation of the mysteries of Christ as they were presented in the perennial cycle of the Liturgy.

There is also a very pronounced affective dimension in Marmion's writings that is in keeping with this Benedictine tradition. For him the knowledge of God should lead to the seeking of God, and so in his writings there is as much an appeal to the heart as to the head. He seeks to bring about a deeper understanding and realization of the truths of the faith in order to inflame the heart to renewed dedication and service. Thus, interspersed in his conferences are frequent prayers. Marmion writes as a man of faith and prayer for those who approach his writings in this same spirit.

Mention should also be made of the simplicity, clarity and directness that marks everything he wrote. As one writer stresses: "In nothing is Dom .Marmion so characteristically a son of St. Benedict than in the simplicity and purity with which like St. Benedict, he transmits to us the fundamental doctrine of Christianity."[8]

# II

Let us turn to a closer look at the main themes in Marmion's spirituality. In general, we can say that his major emphasis is on our divine adoption through Jesus Christ. In our consideration here, let us first consider his teaching on God's divine plan of adoption for us; secondly, the centrality of Christ in all of Marmion's spiritual conferences; and thirdly the application of this doctrine of our supernatural adoption in Christ to the actual living out of the Christian life.

## Divine Adoption

As noted earlier, Marmion begins his synthesis of the spiritual life with St. Paul's message to the Ephesians that we are the adopted children of God through Christ Jesus. Marmion is convinced that this is the most important truth for us and the foundation of our relationship with God. Yet, he recognized that there are many who while seeking God, hardly succeed in reaching Him. He feels that there are a number of reasons for this. Some are ignorant of the divine plan and thus have no precise idea of what holiness is. Others set aside the divine plan, and make holiness consist in a conception formed by their own mind, and thus wish to be their own guides. Others may have a clear notion of details but lack a synthesis and thus can seem to be constantly going over the same ground. Thus, for Marmion, it is essential that we know as perfectly as possible the divine idea of holiness. What, then, is God's plan for us?

It is God's plan that we share in His own life, that we participate in the divine life through the grace of supernatural adoption that comes to us through Jesus Christ. With a will infinitely free, but full of love, God has predestined us to be not only creatures but His children. "To us," Marmion writes, "God will give the condition and sweet name of children. By nature God has only one Son; by love, He wills to have an innumerable multitude: that is the *grace of supernatural adoption.*"[9]

Participation in this divine life is brought about by grace. God's grace becomes the principle of the divine life in us and raises us to a supernatural union with Him, a union and a relationship that exceeds the capacities, the strength and the exigencies of our nature.

This plan was first realized in Adam from the dawn of creation but later crossed by sin. The divine plan was restored, however, by a marvelous intervention of love and mercy. The Son of God, who dwells eternally in the bosom of the Father, unites Himself in time to a human nature, and through His redeeming work restores the grace of divine life.

This is the divine plan of our supernatural adoption that Marmion never tires of extolling for God's glory. As he summarizes it:

> Such is then in its majestic range and merciful simplicity God's plan for us. *God wills our holiness.* He wills it because He loves us infinitely, and we ought

to will it with Him. He wills to make us saints *in
making us participate in His very life*, and for that end,
*He adopts us as His children*, and the heirs of His
infinite glory and eternal beatitude. *Grace* is
the principle of this holiness, supernatural in its
source, in its acts, and in its fruits. But God only gives
us this adoption *through His Son*, Jesus Christ. It is
in Him, and by Him, that God wills to unite Himself
to us, and that we should be united to Him. Christ is
the Way, the only way, to lead us to God, and without
Him we can do nothing. Our holiness has no other
foundation than that same one which God has established, that is to say, union with Jesus Christ.[10]

### Centrality of Christ

The role of Christ in this plan is clear. "We are here at the
central point of the Divine Plan," Marmion writes. "*It is from
Jesus Christ, it is through Jesus Christ that we receive the Divine
adoption.*"[11]    Here Marmion is echoing St. Paul's teaching
on Christ and nothing is as clear and decisive in his thought.
Christ is the Way, leading us to God, and without Him we
can do nothing. Christ Jesus is the only Way, the only Truth,
the only Life. For Marmion, the great grace is to understand
"that Christ is our All, that He is the *Alpha* and *Omega*, that
out of Him we have nothing, that in Him we have everything, for everything is summed up in Him."[12]

As we have seen, Marmion also stresses that we can only
be saints according to the measure in which the life of Christ
is in us. This is the only holiness God asks of us and there is
no other. We can only be holy in Jesus Christ:

Such is the very source of our holiness. As everything in Jesus Christ can be summed up in His

Divine Sonship, thus everything in the Christian can be summed up in his participation of this sonship, by Jesus Christ, and in Jesus Christ. *Our holiness is nothing else but this: the more we participate in the Divine life through the communication Jesus Christ makes to us of the grace of which He ever possesses the fullness, the higher is the degree of our holiness.* All the holiness God has destined for our souls has been placed in the Humanity of Christ, and it is from this source that we must draw.[13]

St. Paul is also a special guide for Marmion in his book, *Christ in His Mysteries*. He realizes that for St. Paul, all is summed up in the practical knowledge of the mystery of Christ. St. Paul's mission was essentially to preach Christ, and Christ crucified, and to make known to all the faithful that "in Christ we find all." Marmion writes that "in Christ alone can be found all the 'wisdom, and justice and sanctification, and redemption' (1 Cor 1:30) of which souls have need in all ages. And this is why St. Paul makes the whole formation of the inward man consist in the practical knowledge of the mystery of Jesus."[14]

For Marmion, there is an intimate connection between our growth in Christ and the contemplation of His mysteries:

The more we know Christ, the more we enter deeply into the mysteries of His Person and of His life, the more we study, in prayer, the circumstances and details that Revelation had given to us, the more also will our piety be true and our holiness real.[15]

Thus our knowledge of Christ grows as we enter more deeply into the mysteries of His life. These mysteries of

Jesus are ours as much as they are His. Christ lives them for us and in all of them He shows Himself to us as our model. Also in His mysteries, Christ makes us one with Him as members of His body.

If we are to benefit from the power of Christ's mysteries, we must place ourselves in contact with them. Participation in the mysteries of Christ requires our cooperation. This contact comes first of all from the prayerful reading of the Gospels. It also comes by associating ourselves with the Church in her liturgy. And we must constantly keep in mind that if we are to derive full benefit from the contemplation of Christ's mysteries, we must approach them with faith, reverence, and especially love. For it is love, above all, that is revealed and shines out in the mysteries of Jesus. And it is by love that we understand them.[16]

*Application to Christian Life*

As we review the doctrinal and scriptural foundations of Marmion's spirituality, it is important to keep in mind that the main thrust in his spiritual theology is the actual living out of the Christian life. Through his apostolic work, he was in constant touch with those who were seeking to grow in holiness and in union with God. He conducted many retreats, particularly for religious, and he was constantly engaged as a spiritual director. Thus, in his writings there are present the qualities of realism and practicality. He wrote in terms of practical spiritual need and not on a more theoretical plane. The doctrine was expounded and explained carefully so that it could be realized more fully and put into practice more seriously. Growth in the life of Christ, growth in holiness was his goal.

This holiness for Marmion, as noted before, lies in the actual living out of God's plan for our sanctification. It lies in receiving the divine life from Christ and through Christ, in preserving it and constantly increasing it by an ever closer union with Him who is its source. Marmion writes: "That is why all our spiritual life ought to be based on this fundamental truth: all the work of perfection ought to consist in faithfully safeguarding our participation in the divine Sonship of Jesus and in developing it in the greatest possible manner."[17]

In *Christ the Life of the Soul*, Marmion also stresses that "it will serve for little if it is only in an abstract and theoretical manner that we contemplate this Divine plan. . . . We must *adapt ourselves practically to this plan* under penalty of not belonging to Christ's kingdom."[18]   In the second part of this book, Marmion seeks to explain how to do this. He entitles this section "Foundation and Double Aspect of the Christian Life."

It is faith that is the foundation of the Christian life, faith in the divinity of Jesus Christ who is the source of holiness. To faith must be joined the sacrament of baptism for it is the sacrament of divine adoption, the sacrament by which we truly become the children of God and are incorporated with Christ. Baptism involves a death to sin and a living for Christ, and for Marmion "Christian life is nothing else but the progressive and continuous development, the practical application, throughout our whole life, of this double supernatural result of 'death' and 'life' produced by Baptism."[19]   This supernatural life must be maintained in us by human acts that are "animated by sanctifying grace, and referred to God through charity."[20]   St. Paul's expression "doing the truth in charity" sums up much for Marmion in this regard.

Thus, we must allow the supernatural life in us to grow, to progress, to unfold, and to become perfect. The principal means for the growth and fruition of this life Marmion found in the sacraments, especially the Eucharist, as well as in prayer and the exercise of the virtues, particularly the command to love one another.

The same desire to make practical application of God's divine plan for us marks two of Marmion's other books, *Christ the Ideal of the Monk*,[21] and *Christ the Ideal of the Priest*.[22] The first gives a general view of the monastic idea and institution and then develops the program to be carried out by those who seek to respond to Christ's call to leave all things and follow Him in the monastic life. *Christ the Ideal of the Priest* first focuses on Christ, the author of the priesthood and the priest's sanctity, and then sets out to expound the path to priestly sanctity.

# III

It should come as no surprise from what we have seen up to this point that prayer will be very important for Marmion in his treatment of the spiritual life. He stresses the importance of prayer for all Christians, for he realizes that we must be men and women of prayer if we are to live in truth.[23] When Marmion speaks about the constancy and the steadfastness of the saints in seeking and loving God, he finds the secret of this in their lives of prayer. The person that leads a life of prayer remains united to God, for the fruit of prayer is the firm adherence to God:

> To live a life of prayer is to abide habitually in contact with God in faith, and, in this union, the soul finds the necessary life and strength to do the Divine good pleasure in all things. And as God is for it the

principle of all holiness, the soul that lives by prayer finds in this habitual union with God who created prayer the fruitfulness of its supernatural light.[24]

In speaking of the importance of prayer, Marmion also stresses that it is prayer that enables us to partake with greater fruit of the other means of grace. The one who is given to prayer profits more from the sacraments and the other means of salvation than another whose prayer is without constancy and intensity. Again this is because the principal author of our perfection and holiness is God Himself and it is prayer that keeps one in frequent contact with God.[25]

*Nature of Prayer*

For Marmion, it is our divine adoption, our status as children of God through the grace of Christ that determines our fundamental attitude in prayer. We learn from Christ Himself, who taught us to pray the "Our Father," that "the first and fundamental disposition we must have in our relations with God is that of a child in the presence of his father."[26]   Prayer is the privilege of those whom the Lord has adopted as His children. Thus Marmion defines prayer as "the intercourse of a child of God with his heavenly Father under the action of the Holy Spirit."[27]   It is the expression, under the action of the Holy Spirit, of the sentiments that result from our divine adoption in Jesus Christ.

In developing his reflections on the nature of prayer, Marmion recalls that in conversation one both listens and speaks. After noting that to listen to God and receive His light, it is enough if the heart is filled with faith, reverence, humility, ardent confidence and generous love, Marmion goes on to focus more on the aspect of speaking in prayer:

In order to speak to God, it is necessary to have something to say to Him. What is to be the subject of the conversation? That depends principally on two elements: *the measure of grace* that Christ Jesus gives to the soul, and *the state of the soul* itself.[28]

The first element, then, that must be taken into account is the measure of grace communicated by Christ. Marmion has great sensitivity to individual needs and conditions and he realizes that care must always be taken so as not to impose indiscriminately upon every person one way rather than another. Methods and ways of praying vary for different persons and so we find him writing:

It is then for each and every soul to study for themselves first of all what is the best manner for them of conversing with God. They should, on the one hand, consider their aptitudes, their dispositions, tastes, aspirations, and kind of life, and seek to know the attraction of the Holy Spirit, besides taking into account the progress they have made in spiritual ways. On the other hand, they should be generously docile to the grace of God and the action of the Holy Spirit. Once the best way is found, after some inevitable trials at the beginning, they should keep faithfully to it, until the Holy Spirit draws them into another way. This is, for them, the condition of gaining fruit from their prayers.[29]

Method in prayer, then, must not be confused with the essence of prayer. Methods ought to vary according to individual aptitudes and needs, while prayer in the ordinary sense remains substantially the same for every person for it is "an intercourse in which the child of God pours out his soul before the Heavenly Father, and listens to Him in order to please Him."[30]

The second element that must be taken into account, according to Marmion, is the particular state or stage in which persons find themselves as they seek to grow in the Christian life. He develops his thought here in connection with the traditional stages or ways of the spiritual life, the purgative way, the illuminative way and the unitive way.

For example, in the discursive way, the way of beginners, it will be the discursive element that will ordinarily predominate. Thus, the storing up of intellectual principles and increasing the knowledge of one's faith will be very important. Yet Marmion insists that the purely discursive work should not be confused with prayer. It is the useful and necessary introduction that enlightens, guides and sustains the intelligence. For Marmion,

> prayer only really begins at the moment when
> the will, set on fire with love, enters supernaturally
> into contact with the Divine Good, yielding itself
> lovingly to God in order to please Him and fulfill His
> precept and desire. It is in the heart that prayer
> essentially dwells.[31]

Marmion recognizes, too, that the more a person advances in spiritual ways, the more the discursive work of reasoning is reduced.

In the illuminative way, the stage of those advancing in the spiritual life, it will be the contemplation of the mysteries of Christ that will take on great importance. The most direct way of knowing God at this stage, Marmion teaches, is looking at Our Lord and contemplating His actions and words. For this reason, it is very important for persons who desire to live by prayer to read the Gospels constantly so that

the words of Christ might abide in them and become principles of life. It is also very helpful to follow the Church's
liturgical cycle which represents the actions of Jesus and
recalls His words. We have here abundant food for prayer,
and in all of this it is the Holy Spirit that makes us understand these words and all they contain.

In the following passage, Marmion summarizes well this
prayerful stance to Christ's life and words:

> When we are every day faithful to consecrate a time,
> longer or shorter according to our aptitudes and
> duties of state, in speaking with our Heavenly
> Father, in gathering up His inspirations and listen-
> ing to what the Holy Spirit 'brings to mind', then the
> words of Christ . . . go on multiplying, inundating
> the soul with Divine Light and opening out in it
> fountains of life so that the soul's thirst may be ever
> assuaged. In this is realized the promise of Christ
> Jesus: that if any man should thirst, and come to
> Him and drink there should spring up within him
> that believeth 'rivers of living water.'[32]

\*   \*   \*   \*   \*   \*   \*

Such is the legacy of Dom Marmion, abbot of the Benedictine monastery of Maredsous. It is a rich one, indeed,
because it draws deeply from the scriptural and doctrinal
founts of the faith. Without in any way attempting to be
novel or original, his conferences have these qualities because of the clarity, directness and simplicity with which they
come forth. They are written in a spirit of faith and prayer
that seeks to let the message speak for itself. As he was in his
own lifetime, so too in his writings, Columba Marmion

continues to be a solid guide who seeks to lead others to a
deeper appreciation and love of Christ who is the life of the
soul.

1 Dom Raymond Thibaut, *Columba Marmion, A Master of the Spiritual Life*
(London: Sands & Co., 1932), pp. 376-377.
2 Columba Marmion, *Christ the Life of the Soul* (St. Louis: B. Herder Book Co.,
1925), p. 13.
3 Marmion quotes this passage from Ephesians, 1:4-6 at the beginning of *Christ
the Life of the Soul*, p. 21.
4 Thibaut, pp. 22-24.
5 Marmion's integration of theology and spirituality has often been noted. e.g.
"Seldom does one find so beautiful a synthesis of the Christian dogmas in their
relation with the spiritual life." cf. Thibaut, p. 362.
6 Marmion writes: "When we study attentively the Epistles of St. Paul, it is
evident that for him all is summed up in the practical knowledge of Christ." Cf.
*Christ in His Mysteries* (St. Louis: Herder , 1939), p. 3.
7 *Ibid.*, p. 8.
8 See the article "Benedictine Influence in the Doctrine of Abbot Marmion" by
Fr. Eugene Boylan in *Abbot Marmion, An Irish Tribute* (Cook: The Mercier Press,
1948), p. 47.
9 *Christ the Life of the Soul*, p. 24.
10 *Ibid.*, p. 38.
11 *Ibid.*, p. 35.
12 *Ibid.*, p. 44. In his development of Christ as the source of our sanctification
Marmion, following St. Thomas Aquinas, speaks of Christ as the exemplary
cause, the meritorious cause and the efficient cause of our holiness. He
develops all these points carefully in this book.
13 *Ibid.*, p. 38.
14 *Christ in His Mysteries*, p. 6.
15 *Ibid.*, p. 9.
16 *Ibid.*, p. 29.
17 *Ibid.*, p. 55.
18 *Christ the Life of the Soul*, p. 132.
19 *Ibid.*, p. 162.
20 *Ibid.*, p. 204.
21 Columba Marmion, *Christ the Ideal of the Monk* (St. Louis: Herder, 1926).
22 Columba Marmion, *Christ the Ideal of the Priest* (St. Louis: Herder, 1952).
23 Marmion writes: "Now it is, above all, in our prayers that we acknowledge and
proclaim the total subordination before God in which we pass our life." *Christ
the Ideal of the Priest*, p. 242.

24 *Christ the Ideal of the Monk*, p. 338.
25 *Christ the Life of the Soul*, p. 301.
26 *Ibid.*, p. 304.
27 *Ibid.*, p. 302.
28 *Ibid.*, p. 307.
29 *Ibid.*, p. 309.
30 *Ibid.*
31 *Ibid.*, p. 311.
32 *Ibid.*, p. 314.

# John Henry
# NEWMAN (1801-1890)

JOHN HENRY NEWMAN was a giant of a man in many ways. He was richly endowed with intellectual, spiritual and personal gifts and talents, and was truly one of the religious genuises of modern times. His great learning and simple and sincere piety were blended in a way that proved to be extremely attractive to others and a source of great influence upon those who came across him personally or through his writings. Greatly esteemed and honored during his long life of almost ninety years, he continues to be very influential today. He was truly a seminal thinker who was ahead of his times in many ways.

Newman always led a very active life. It has become almost a truism to speak of the "manysidedness" of his life and work since he was involved in so many activities. He was at various times a parish priest, a teacher, a well-known preacher and lecturer, a writer, an editor of magazines, an organizer and director of a school for boys, the founder and religious superior of the Oratorians in England, the head of a new university, and a cardinal of the Roman Catholic Church. All of these activities were directed to the service of God and the cause of revealed religion. Singularly absent were any personal ambitions and desires for prestige and honor.

His vast writings include autobiographies, biographies, poems, novels, tracts, essays, sermons, controversial polemics, dialogues, histories, open letters, lectures, treatises, editorial commentaries and prefaces. Newman always brought a special creative quality to his writings and they are all marked by a richness and depth of content and a clarity and brilliance in style. Newman's mastery of the English language stands forth on every page.

The focus here will be on Newman's spirituality and prayer. His spirituality does not constitute any separate segment of his writings but is found integrated with his overall religious thought. Newman's own faith and love of God shine forth on every page he wrote. A rich source of his spirituality, however, can be found in the many sermons he preached over the years. The sermons he preached while still an Anglican at St. Mary's Church, Oxford, over a period of fifteen years (1828-1843) are a particularly rich source.[1]

This essay will first consider some of the significant events in Newman's life and his personal experiences of God that throw light on his spirituality. Secondly, it will consider some of the general aspects of his spirituality and the themes he emphasizes. Finally, some of his reflections on prayer will be considered in light of these points.

# *I*

Newman was the eldest of six children and he grew up in what seemed to be a closely knit family. He was brought up as an Anglican and his early years were basically tranquil and serene. At the age of fifteen he went through a period of scepticism but a religious experience followed which had a profound and lasting influence upon him and his relationship with God. Newman never attempted to describe this conversion experience in which "Thy wonderful grace turned me right around" as he was later to write. But it left him with a profound conviction of God's existence and his relationship to Him and a deep awareness of the reality of the unseen world. He was also left with the certainty of his own election and the conviction that God was calling him to the celibate state.

This experience was followed by an Evangelical fervor that continued during his early years at Oxford. After his election as a Fellow of Oriel College at Oxford, his religious commitment and spiritual life continued to deepen. This move, however, led to a significant broadening of his religious views as he was gradually weaned away from his Evangelical leaning and brought into fuller contact with the traditional teachings and doctrines of the Catholic faith.[2]

Note should be made here of another religious experience that had much significance for Newman. It occurred during what is often referred to as a period of creative pause in his life. In the winter of 1833, Newman took a trip to the Mediterranean with his close friend Hurrell Froude and Froude's father. After visiting Malta and Rome with them, Newman went on to Sicily by himself when the Froudes returned to England. He was stricken with a fever in Sicily and lay close to death for days, cared for and attended only by his Italian guide. Newman later wrote his "My Sickness in Sicily" in which he described his feelings at this time. He felt penitent and self-reproachful at the aspects of willfulness he found in himself. He felt hollow, like a mirror which remains cold while heat passes through it. Yet he was convinced he "had not sinned against light" and he was renewed in his sense of God's providence and the divine call. He was convinced, too, that he would not die at this time for he sensed God had some work for him in England.[3]

This purification by illness and intuitive self-knowledge led to a peace and surrender to God's will that found expression in his "Lead, Kindly Light," one of his best known poems. Newman composed this poem (originally entitled "The Pillar of the Cloud") at sea while returning home. Since it sums up so much of Newman's maturing spirituality, it would be helpful to quote it here.

> Lead, Kindly Light, amid the encircling gloom
>     Lead Thou me on!
> The night is dark, and I am far from home —
>     Lead Thou me on!
> Keep Thou my feet; I do not ask to see
> The distant scene — one step enough for me.
>
> I was not ever thus, nor pray'd that Thou
>     Shouldst lead me on.
> I loved to choose and see my path, but now
>     Lead Thou me on.
> I loved the garish day, and, spite of fears,
> Pride ruled my will: remember not past years.
>
> So long Thy power hath blest me, sure it still
>     Will lead me on,
> O'er moor and fen, o'er crag and torrent, till
>     The night is gone;
> And with the morn those angel faces smile
> Which I have loved long since, and lost awhile.[4]

Newman returned to England renewed in spirit and ready to throw himself with enthusiasm into the Oxford Movement which was just commencing. This was basically a religious renewal movement within the Anglican Church. A spiritual lethargy had cast itself over the Establishment and Newman and others saw that its spiritual vitality was being threatened by rationalistic and liberalistic tendencies in the Church. The leaders of the movement sought to counter the superficial religion of the day with a return to the sources of the Faith — to Sacred Scripture and the teaching of the Fathers. Newman led the way, particularly through the various "Tracts for the Times" he wrote and the preaching he did Sunday after Sunday from the pulpit at St. Mary's.

The "Via Media" Newman attempted to maintain could not be sustained as the passage of time brought strong opposition from certain sections of the Anglican Church and increasing self-doubts about his own position. The appearance of his Tract Ninety brought things to a head and it was not long before he resigned his pulpit and quietly retired to Littlemore. The final break with the Anglican Church was inevitable and in 1843 Newman preached his difficult and poignant sermon, "The Parting of Friends."

Although Newman had left the Anglican Church, he was not yet ready to embrace Roman Catholicism. It was a time of waiting and searching as he sought God's will in his life. He was joined at Littlemore for this time of prayer and study by such companions as John Dalgairns, William Lockhart and Ambrose St. John, and during this time of waiting and searching they formed a quasi-religious community. In 1845, Newman finished his important *Essay on the Development of Christian Doctrine*, and shortly after that he made the final move to Rome.

Newman was in his mid forties when he embraced Roman Catholicism. Approximately 45 more years would stretch out before him as a Catholic. They were to be full and busy years as he continued the energetic activity that marked his years as an Anglican. His writing and lecturing would continue and he would be asked to assume challenging and important responsibilities. In many respects they were not easy years for him. There were many successes, to be sure, but there were also defeats and disappointments and he often found himself at the center of conflicts.[5]

The decade between 1853 and 1863 was a particularly difficult period for Newman as so many of his hopes and dreams failed to materialize. The Catholic University in Ireland which he founded and served as rector for a number of years did not turn out as he hoped. He was also pained by the difficulties and conflicts that emerged in his own religious community. As the Founder of the Oratory in England, he felt a certain responsibility for the tension that developed between the Birmingham and London Oratories and for their ultimate separation. Also, an article of his "On Consulting the Faithful on Matters of Doctrine" was related to Rome and this matter was not cleared up for a number of years.

Newman felt these and other disappointments keenly and we find him expressing a sense of discouragement and failure in a journal dating from 1863. He was over sixty years old at this time and he wondered what he had accomplished since his move to Rome. Yet it was a mark of his greatness that throughout these difficult years Newman remained firm and steadfast in his faith. His spirit of hope and trust in God's providential love remained the strong foundation of his life as he sought to serve his Creator with faith and humility.

The publication of his *Apologia Pro Vita Sua* in 1863 was a turning point for Newman. It was warmly and enthusiastically received by both Catholics and Anglicans and it restored him to a position of great influence in the English Church. It somehow seemed to exorcise the spectre of failure which had haunted him during the preceding years. Although there would still be certain conflicts and disappointments, his latter years were marked by many honors and expressions of esteem. He continued to be a source of great influence, particularly through his writings. His elevation to the cardinalate in 1879 by Pope Leo XIII was a particular source of consolation to the aging Newman, as it seemed "to lift the cloud from him forever." Death came at the age of 89 at the Oratory in Birmingham on August 11, 1890.

## II

Newman's spirituality and his spirit of prayer were so intimately connected with his own life that it seemed necessary to give some overview of his life first. With this background, let us turn to some of the general aspects of his spirituality. This will be followed by a consideration of the major themes of his spiritual thought.

The element of integration stands out in Newman's spirituality. His spirituality forms no separate segment of his life and writings but is thoroughly integrated with both. Newman in his own day was not looked upon as a spiritual writer in the restricted sense. Perhaps his other gifts and activities overshadowed this aspect; perhaps this title was associated more with Father Faber and some of the London Oratorians. But spiritual writer he was indeed. Christian spirituality was an abiding concern for him and his spiritual teaching is found throughout his writings. As we have already noted, his many published sermons are the richest source of his spirituality.

His particular theory of the role and responsibility of the tutor should be noted in connection with the aspect of integration. Newman had strong views on this subject as attested by his ongoing dispute with the provost while he was tutoring at Oxford. Newman always looked upon tutoring as a profoundly religious activity. For him it involved the spiritual as well as the intellectual formation of the student.

Turning to the main sources of Newman's spirituality, priority has to be given to Sacred Scripture. As Newman tells us at the beginning of his *Apologia*, he "was brought up from a child to take great delight in reading ·the Bible."[6] This knowledge and love of the Bible continued to deepen throughout his life and as a result his spiritual doctrine was continually nourished by the teaching of Scripture. It is interesting also to note the insightful and effective way he makes use of the various Old and New Testament figures to illustrate the development of his thought in his sermons.

Secondly, the Fathers of the Church are a rich source of his spiritual thought. During his early years as a Fellow of Oriel College at Oxford, his systematical reading of the Fathers not only led to the publication of *The Arians of the Fourth Century* in 1833, but also left him with a deep knowledge and profound love for the Patristic writings.

In addition to the Biblical and Patristic influences, there is also a very strong doctrinal element in Newman's spirituality. There is a definite inclusiveness in Newman's spiritual thought and an expansiveness in the doctrines treated. He never limits himself to certain aspects of Christian revelation but teaches and preaches the Faith in its fullness and richness.

He preached the Christian truths as the basis for a life of holiness. His spiritual teaching was simply the Christian faith, as something to be both believed and lived. Newman realized that religion becomes a vital and energizing force only when a person is constantly aware of Christian dogmas, not as abstract truths, but as concrete realities that call for a sincere and personal response.

Newman's purpose and methodology should be kept in mind at this point. He was facing a Christianity of the day which appeared inauthentic and formalistic in many ways. He describes it in such sermons as "Religion of the Day" and "The Religion of the Pharisee." Although it had many good and solid values, it had accomodated itself to the spirit of the day. It could be lived without reference to Christ, grace and the sacraments, and it avoided many of the more demanding and challenging aspects of the Gospel message. Newman set himself in opposition to this watered down type of Christianity and sought to present the Faith in its fullness and richness. He sought to build up the Church by restoring to it the purity of doctrine and holiness of the early Apostolic Church. He urged his listeners to live their faith with the utmost seriousness and sincerity.

Newman's first published sermon is entitled "Holiness Necessary for Future Blessedness." This sets the tone for the rest of his sermons. Holiness was the object of Newman's preaching, teaching and personal direction. It should be kept in mind, too, that Newman's spiritual teaching is directed primarily to the laity, to those who came to hear him preach week after week, year after year. Although it was a general audience, it was composed of people who were serious about the practice of their faith, and in no way did Newman limit or water down the demands of the Christian message. Newman's spirituality was a demanding and challenging one. He called for the fullest and sincerest response — a response which placed Christ and His word at the center of one's life.

In connection with the strong doctrinal flavor in Newman's spirituality, we might recall the importance he always gave to the concept of "realization." His fuller treatment of "notional" and "real" knowledge is contained in his *Grammar of Assent* where he treats the larger question of "real assent." However, in the sermons he often describes the process whereby abstract or "notional" knowledge is changed into "real" knowledge. Realization involves opening one's mind to a truth, in the sense of bringing the truth into one's consciousness, dwelling upon it, contemplating it vividly and bringing it home to oneself. It involves opening one's heart to a truth and responding with one's entire being. Knowledge is then no longer abstract but becomes an influential principle within the person leading to a number of consequences both in opinion and in conduct. It was to this realization and concrete assimilation of the mysteries of the faith that Newman sought to lead his listeners. As one writer summarizes it:

> Newman's purpose in the sermons, then, was to lead men to realize vividly for themselves the mysteries of faith, to comprehend authentic Christianity as a concrete way of life, not merely as an abstract programme for living. Christian doctrine and morality were presented in a way that demanded an authentic response, a definite commitment of the entire being.[7]

# *III*

Let us turn now to consideration of some of the themes Newman emphasizes in his spirituality. The reality of God and of the unseen world must first be highlighted. We might recall again Newman's experience at the age of fifteen when he was left with an overwhelming conviction of two things: the existence of God and the existence of himself. In the *Apologia* Newman speaks of being confirmed at this time "in my mistrust of the reality of material phenomena, and making me rest in the thought of two and two only supreme and luminously self-evident beings, myself and my Creator."[8]

The reality of God and of the unseen world remained strong and vibrant throughout Newman's long life. He himself strove to be faithful to these realities and he urged others to be steadfast in clinging to them. He had a great power to awaken in others the awareness of the unseen world and in his preaching, teaching and writing, he strove to bring them to a deeper realization. Realist that he was, he knew that these realities had to be nourished by prayer and the other means that foster an awareness of God in one's life. For example, speaking of a person who had difficulty in grasping doctrinal truths, Newman writes:

> Let him but act as if the next world were before him, let him but give himself to such devotional exercises as we ought to observe in the presence of an Almighty, All-Holy, and All-Merciful God, and it will be a rare case indeed if his difficulties do not vanish.[9]

In Newman's mind, if persons are convinced of God's reality, they will realize all that flows from that conviction, particularly their contingency and dependence upon God:

> We are not our own, any more than what we possess is our own. We did not make ourselves; we cannot be supreme over ourselves. We cannot be our own masters. We are God's property by creation, by redemption, by regeneration. He has a triple claim upon us. Is it not our happiness thus to view the matter? Is it any happiness, or any comfort, to consider that we *are* our own?. . . . No, we are creatures; and as being such, we have two duties, to be resigned and to be thankful.[10]

Closely connected with this strong awareness of God's reality and the reality of the unseen world was the abiding sense of God's providence that Newman had throughout his life. It was continually operative in his own life and intimately connected with his sense of divine mission. We have noted the importance of Newman's illness in Sicily and the strong sense of God's providential love that accompanied it. His conviction that in God's divine plan some work was awaiting him in England led to his certainty that he would not die at this time. Newman expresses this sense of hope and trust in one of his meditations where he writes:

> God has created me to do Him some definite service;
> He has committed some work to me which He has
> not committed to another. I have my mission — I
> never may know it in this life, but I shall be told it in
> the next. . . . Therefore I will trust Him. Whatever,
> wherever, I am, I can never be thrown away. If I am
> in sickness, my sickness may serve Him; in per-
> plexity, my perplexity may serve Him; if I am in
> sorrow, my sorrow may serve Him.[11]

Foremost in Newman's mind was the desire to be faithful to his mission and to God's will unfolding in his life. With great simplicity and sincerity he sought to focus on God leading him on in His service. He brings this out very clearly and poignantly in his last sermon as an Anglican when he stood at a crossroad of his life. In this sermon, "The Parting of Friends," he prays at the end:

> And, O my brethren, O kind and affectionate hearts,
> O loving friends, should you know any one whose lot
> it has been, by writing or by word of mouth, in some
> degree to help you thus to act; if he has ever told you

what you knew about yourselves, or what you did not
know; has read to you your wants or feelings, and
comforted you by the very reading; has made you
feel that there was a higher life than this daily one,
and a brighter world than that you see; or encouraged you, or sobered you, or opened a way to
the inquiring or soothed the perplexed; if what he
has said or done has ever made you take interest
in him, and feel well inclined towards him; remember such a one in time to come, though you
hear him not, and pray for him, that in all things, he
may know God's will, and at all times he may be
ready to fulfill it.[12]

This desire was to be severely tested in the years ahead,
particularly during the difficult years of 1853-1863 when a
sense of failure and discouragement hung over him. Yet
throughout this period Newman remained patient and
steadfast in his faith in God's providence. His hope rested
not on the apparent success or failure of his undertakings
but on the God in whose light he sought to walk.

In one of his sermons, "Remembrance of Past Mercies,"
Newman reflects on God's providence as exemplified by the
patriarch Jacob. In Newman's mind, Jacob's distinguishing
grace was "a habit of affectionate musing upon God's provi-
dences towards him in times past, and of overflowing thankfulness for them." It is this same spirit he urges on us as he
writes:

Well were it for us, if we had the character of mind
instanced in Jacob, and enjoined on his descendants;
the temper of dependence upon God's providence,
and thankfulness under it, and careful memory of all
He had done for us. It would be well if we were in

the habit of looking at all we have as God's gift, undeservedly given, and day by day continued to us solely by His mercy.[13]

Let us then view God's providence towards us more religiously than we have hitherto done. Let us try to gain a truer view of what we are, and where we are in His kingdom. Let us humbly and reverently attempt to trace His guiding hand in the years which we have hitherto lived. Let us thankfully commemorate the many mercies He has vouchsafed to us in time past, the many sins He has not remembered, the many dangers He has averted, the many prayers He has answered, the many mistakes He has corrected, the many warnings, the many lessons, the much light, the abounding comfort which He has from time to time given. Le us dwell upon times and seasons, times of trouble, times of joy, times of trial, times of refreshment.[14]

Christian repentance is also a very important theme in Newman's spirituality. He speaks of it often in such terms as "self-surrender," "self-deceit," "a willingness to be changed," etc. Some have found him somewhat stern and over-earnest in this area, but Newman himself would see it as the clear recognition of the demands of Christian perfection. And it was Christian perfection and holiness that Newman was constantly setting before his listeners. He stresses that a Christian is called to live in simplicity and sincerity, with a single and innocent heart, illuminated and guided by God's grace. Walking before God in simplicity and sincerity is for Newman the same as serving God with what Scripture refers to as "a perfect heart." Following the testimony of his conscience, "man serves with a perfect heart, who serves God in all parts of his duty; and, not here and there, but here and there and everywhere; not perfectly as regards the quality of his obedience, but perfectly as regards its extent; not completely, but consistently."[15]

Newman recognizes, however, that this does not come easily to our fallen natures. There is a principle of self-seeking that works against the process of letting go and allowing ourselves to be changed: "What then is it that we who profess religion lack? I repeat it, this: a willingness to be changed, a willingness to suffer (if I may use such a word), to suffer Almighty God to change us. We do not like to let go our old selves."[16]

The words "hypocrisy" and "surrender" appear often in this context in Newman's spirituality. They represent two opposing stances or attitudes before God.

The first, "hypocrisy," is a major obstacle to union with God and a life of holiness. For Newman "a hypocrite is one who professes to be serving God faithfully, while he serves Him in only some part of his duty, not all parts."[17] Thus there is a lack of simplicity and a reserve or holding back in some area or areas. While not wishing to be separated from God, while even trying to serve Him earnestly, we yet will not give up our old selves.

Hypocrisy for Newman also manifests itself as insincerity or self-deceit. This self-deceit can manifest itself in the areas of secret faults, our relations with others, and in our relations with God. Newman's method of dealing with this hypocrisy is through careful self-reflection. Although it is certainly introspective, it is not meant to be any kind of morbid self-reflection, but rather a process that leads to a healthy self-knowledge. For Newman, self-knowledge is the key to the Gospel and to the realization of its truth.

The term "surrender" sums up for Newman the way to perfection, all that is most fundamental, most generous, and exacting in the Gospel. For example, he speaks of it as "the one and only way of salvation and perfection."[18]    He also writes: "But when a man comes to God to be saved, then, I say, the essence of true conversion is a *surrender* of himself, an unreserved, unconditional surrender."[19]    Surrender, then, for Newman is the giving up of all reserve. It is a spirit of simplicity and sincerity before God. It is a willingness to fall into God's hands and to be changed. It is an unlocking of the heart to God without defense, without excuse.

The final theme in Newman's spirituality that we will mention here is the doctrine of the Indwelling of the Blessed Trinity. Newman felt that this was little understood and often neglected, and so he stressed it constantly. Entire sermons are devoted to this subject such as "The Indwelling Spirit" and "The Gift of the Spirit." He sought to bring his listeners to an understanding and a realization of this sublime reality, for he was convinced that true Christians are those who have a ruling sense of God's presence within them.

In his sermon "Righteousness not of us, but in us" Newman recalls that when Christ ascended, He did not leave us to ourselves. Since the work was not yet done, He sent His Spirit. The Spirit came "to finish in us, what Christ had finished in himself but left unfinished as regards us. To Him it is committed to apply to us severally all that Christ had done for us." Newman goes on to write:

> For if all gifts of grace are with the Spirit, and the presence of the Spirit is within us, it follows that these gifts are to be manifested and wrought in us. If Christ is our sole hope, and Christ is given to us by the Spirit, and the Spirit be an inward presence, our sole hope is an inward change. As a light placed in

a room pours out its rays on all sides, so the presence
of the Holy Ghost imbues us with life, strength,
holiness, love, acceptableness, righteousness.[20]

# *IV*

An important source of Newman's legacy of prayer is his
own prayers, meditations and devotions that were collected
and published after his death in a book entitled *Meditations
and Devotions.* This rich source includes meditations on the
Litany of Loretto for the month of May; novenas and
litanies in honor of St. Philip Neri; meditations on the
Stations of the Cross; meditations on Christian doctrine;
and various prayers interspersed with the meditations.

Newman brought a special creative touch to whatever he
turned his hand, and this is particularly true of his prayers
and meditations. His own deep piety and marvelous writing
ability combine to give them a distinct simplicity, directness
and beauty. They reflect a very prayerful person who has
the gift of leading others to God and to personal prayer.
They overflow from a love inspired by awe, admiration,
gratitude and longing for God. Although they are centered
on doctrine, they have the power to open our hearts to God
and help us to speak to God words of praise, adoration,
sorrow and petition. It should be noted, too, that many of
Newman's prayers and verses have been included in the
Roman Breviary and many other prayer books and books of
devotion.

Newman's meditations and devotions (as is true for the
sermons) are meant for the ordinary Christian. There is
nothing restrictive or elitist about them. Although recognizing their importance and value, he leaves to others
the treatment of mystical prayer and other advanced types

of prayer. This flowed from his own preference and basic orientation in the spiritual life. Newman never saw anything extraordinary about his own personal spirituality and prayer. For example, when on one occasion he was asked his advice on the writings of St. John of the Cross, he answered that he did know much of the subject and "being an ordinary Catholic, was content after the New Testament with the Imitation."[21]

In one of his sermons, Newman focuses on communion with God and prayer in what he considers the large sense of the word. He speaks of prayer as *conversing* with God, a divine converse differing from human as God differs from us. We are members of another world and for Newman prayer and praise are the modes of intercourse with this world. "As speech is the organ of human society, and the means of human civilization, so is prayer the instrument of divine fellowship and divine training."[22]    However, just as he who does not use a gift loses it, "he who neglects to pray, not only suspends the enjoyment, but is in a way to lose the possession, of his divine citizenship."[23]

Thus we find Newman stressing the necessity of what he refers to as the habit of prayer, "the practice of turning to God and the unseen world, in every season, in every place, in every emergency."[24]    Newman writes:

But as our bodily life discovers itself by its activity,
so is the presence of the Holy Spirit in us discovered
by a spiritual activity; and this activity is the spirit of
continual prayer. Prayer is to spiritual life what the
beating of the pulse and the drawing of the breath
are to the life of the body. It would be as absurd to
suppose that life could last when the body was cold
and motionless and senseless, as to call a soul alive

which does not pray. The state or habit of spiritual
life exerts itself, consists, in the continual activity of
prayer.[25]

Let us look a little more closely at this concept of "continual prayer" since Newman places such an emphasis upon
it. In one of his sermons entitled "Mental Prayer," Newman
takes as his text the words of St. Paul, "Pray without ceasing." He speaks of two modes of prayer mentioned in
Scripture: one is the prayer of set times and places, and set
forms; the other is what St. Paul's text speaks of, namely
continual or habitual prayer. Newman refers to this second
type of prayer as holding communion with God, or living in
God's sight; this type of prayer may be done "all through the
day, wherever we are, and is commanded us as the duty, or
rather the characteristic, of those who are really servants
and friends of Jesus Christ."[26]

Newman develops the intimate relationship between
continual prayer and the practice of religion as a habit, a
state of mind and a way of life that involves the entire person
continually. In the practice of religion Newman calls for a
genuine wholeness and an earnest sincerity. He develops
this in the following passage in which it is interesting to note
the similarity with St. Ignatius Loyola's concepts of "finding
God in all things" and being "a contemplative in action."

> A man who is religious, is religious morning, noon,
> and night; his religion is a certain character, a mould
> in which his thoughts, words, and actions are cast, all
> forming parts of one and the same whole. He sees
> God in all things; every course of action he directs
> towards those spiritual objects which God has
> revealed to him; every occurrence of the day, every
> event, every person met with, all news which he

hears, he measures by the standard of God's will.
And a person who does this may be said almost
literally to pray without ceasing; for knowing himself to be in God's presence, he is continually led to
address Him reverently, whom he sets always before
him, in the inward language of prayer and praise, of
humble confession and joyful trust.[27]

Newman also stresses the importance of meditation for
the Christian who wishes to have a heart open and responsive to Christ and His Word. He recognizes our failures at
times to be moved and to be impressed. So often we fail to
understand the Gospel; our eyes are dim and our ears are
hard of hearing and we have so little faith. Newman traces
this to a lack of meditation. We do not meditate, and therefore we are not impressed. In words similar to his stress on
continual prayer, he writes:

What is meditating on Christ? It is simply this, thinking habitually and constantly of Him and of His
deeds and sufferings. It is to have Him before
our minds as One whom we may contemplate, worship, and address when we rise up, when we lie
down, when we eat and drink, when we are at home
and abroad, when we are working, or walking, or
at rest, when we are alone, and again when we are in
company; this is meditating. And by this, and
nothing short of this, will our hearts come to feel as
they ought.[28]

Recalling the old dictum, "Out of sight, out of mind,"
Newman realizes it will be the same regarding Christ unless
we make continual efforts to think of Him, His love, His
precepts, His gifts, and His promises. Newman urges us to:

recall to mind what we read in the Gospels and
in holy books about Him; we must bring before us
what we have heard in Church; we must pray God to
enable us to do so, to bless the doing so, and to make
us do so in a simple-minded, sincere, and reverential
spirit. In a word, we must meditate, for all this
is meditation; and this even the most unlearned
person can do, and will do, if he has a will to do it.[29]

Newman also emphasizes that we must have tender,
sensitive, living hearts if we are to be saved. Our hearts must
be broken up like ground, and dug, and watered, and
tended and cultivated, until they become as gardens acceptable to God in which the Lord may walk and dwell. According to Newman, "this change must take place in our hearts if
we would be saved; in a word, we must have what we have
not by nature, faith and love; and how is this to be effected,
under God's grace, but by godly and practical meditation
through the day."[30]

\* \* \* \* \* \* \*

When Newman was raised to the cardinalate in 1879 he
took as his motto the expression "cor ad cor loquitur"
("heart speaks to heart"). This very aptly sums up his spirituality and prayer since they are characterized by directness,
sincerity, and a very personal and concrete approach. His
spirituality is also marked by a sense of oneness and
harmony. Thomas Merton recognized this aspect in one of
his journals, as he reflected on Newman's love for Clement
of Alexandria. Noting Newman's love for music throughout
his life, Merton observes that "all that was best, expressed
itself for him, in terms of music, harmony, oneness,
sound."[31]   There certainly was a oneness in Newman's life

and writings, for everything was directed to the recognition and service of his Creator and Lord. Finally it should be clear that Newman's whole life and all he did was marked by a spirit of steadfastness and faithfulness as he sought to follow God's will and walk humbly before the Light that filled his life and led him on.

---

1  These sermons have been published many times as the *Parochial and Plain Sermons* in 8 volumes. Other published collections of Newman's sermons are: *Sermons on Subjects of the Day; Sermons Preached on Various Occasions: Discourses to Mixed Congregations;* and *Oxford University Sermons.*

2  Newman writes of these developments in the early pages of his *Apologia Pro Vita Sua.*

3  For a fuller account of his sickness in Sicily cf. Hilda Graef's *God and Myself* (New York: Hawthorn Books, Inc., 1968), p. 40 ff.

4  Cf. Newman's *Verses on Various Occasions* (London: Longmans, Green, and Co., 1910), pp. 156-157.

5  His biographer, Meriol Trevor, writes: "It was Newman's curious fate to be in the first part of his life the symbol of Catholicism to Protestants, and in the second the symbol of protest to Catholics — to the majority a justifiable protest, but to the Ultramontanes in London a centre of rebellion and disunity." Cf. her *Newman: Light in Winter* (New York: Doubleday, 1962), p. 7.

6  Cf. Newman's *Apologia Pro Vita Sua* (New York: Image Books, 1956), p. 125.

7  *Realizations. Newman's Own Selection of His Sermons,* edited with an introduction by Vincent Ferrer Blehl, S.J. (London: Darton, Longman & Todd, 1964), p. xiii.

8  *Apologia Pro Vita Sua,* p. 127.

9  *Parochial and Plain Sermons.* 8 volumes. (London: Longman, Green and Co.), IV, p. 231. Hereafter references to these sermons will be cited as PPS.

10  *PPS* V, 83-84.

11  Cf. Newman, *Meditations and Devotions* (Westminster, MD: Christian Classics, 1975), p. 301.

12  Newman, *The Parting of Friends,* (Westminster, MD: Newman Press, 1961), pp. 22-23.

13  *PPS,* V, pp. 82-83.

14  *Ibid.,* p. 84.

15  *PPS,* V, p. 239.

16  *PPS,* V. p. 241. Newman also writes: "To live is to change, to be perfect is to change often." *Essay on the Development of Christian Doctrine* (London: Longmans, Green and Co.), p. 40.

17  *PPS*, V. p. 240.
18  *PPS*, II, p. 82.
19  *PPS*, V, p. 241.
20  *PPS*, V, p. 138.
21  Cf. Robert Hodge, "Cardinal Newman, Contemplative," *Cistercian Studies* XI, 1976, pp. 206-207.
22  *PPS*, IV, pp. 230-231.
23  *PPS*, IV, p. 228.
24  *PPS*, IV, p. 230.
25  *PPS*, VII, p. 209.
26  *PPS*, VII, p. 204.
27  *PPS*, VII, pp. 205-206.
28  *PPS*, VI, p. 41.
29  *PPS*, VI, p. 42.
30  *PPS*, VI, p. 42. Newman also writes: "It is not once thinking of Christ or twice thinking of Christ that will do it. It is only by going on quietly and steadily, with the thought of Him in our mind's eye, that little by little we shall gain something of warmth, light, life, and love." *PPS*, VI, p. 43.
31  Cf. Merton's *Conjectures of a Guilty Bystander* (New York: Image Books, 1968), pp. 187-188.

# SUGGESTIONS FOR FURTHER READING

## DOROTHY DAY

Day, Dorothy. *The Long Loneliness.* New York: Curtis, 1972.
_____. *From Union Square to Rome.* Maryland: Preservation of the
     Faith Press, 1938.
_____. *House of Hospitality.* New York: Sheed and Ward, 1939.
_____. *Loaves and Fishes.* New York: Curtis Books, 1972.
_____. *On Pilgrimage.* Catholic Worker Books, 1948.
_____. *On Pilgrimage: The Sixties.* New York: Curtis Books, 1972.
_____. *Meditations.* Edited by Stanley Vishnewski. New York:
     Newman Press, 1970.
Miller, William D. *A Harsh and Dreadful Love.* New York:
     Liveright, 1973.
_____. *Dorothy Day, a Biography.* San Francisco: Harper and Row,
     1982.
_____. *All is Grace.* New York: Doubleday, 1987.
*The entire issue of the periodical* America *for Nov. 11, 1972 is devoted to
Dorothy Day on the occasion of her 75th birthday.*

## ABRAHAM JOSHUA HESCHEL

Heschel, Abraham Joshua. *Man's Quest for God.* New York:
     Charles Scribner's, 1954.
_____. *Man Is Not Alone.* New York: Harper Torchbooks, 1966.

_____. *God in Search of Man*. New York: Harper Torchbooks, 1966.

_____. *The Prophets*. 2 vols. New York: Harper Torchbooks, 1971.

_____. *The Insecurity of Freedom*. New York: Farrar, Straus, and Giroux, 1965.

_____. *A Passion For Truth*. New York: Farrar, Straus, and Giroux, 1973.

_____. *Between God and Man*. Edited by Fritz A. Rothschild. New York: The Free Press, 1959.

Sherman, Franklin. *The Promise of Heschel*. Philadelphia: Lippincott, 1970.

*The issue of the periodical* America *for March 10, 1973 is devoted to Heschel*.

## THOMAS MERTON

Merton, Thomas. *The Seven Storey Mountain*. New York: Signet Books, 1952.

_____. *The Sign of Jonas*. New York: Image Books, 1956.

_____. *New Seeds of Contemplation*. New York: New Directions, 1961.

_____. *No Man Is An Island*. New York: Image Books, 1967.

_____. *Life and Holiness*. New York: Image Books, 1964.

_____. *Spiritual Direction and Meditation*. Collegeville: Liturgical Press, 1960.

_____. *Conjectures of a Guilty Bystander*. New York: Image Books, 1968.

_____. *Faith and Violence*. University of Notre Dame Press, 1968.

_____. *Contemplative Prayer*. New York: Image Books, 1971.

_____. *Zen and the Birds of Appetite*. New York: New Directions, 1968.

_____. *The Asian Journal of Thomas Merton*. New York: New Directions, 1968.

_____. *Thomas Merton On Peace*. With an introduction by Gordon C. Zahn. New York: McCall Publishing Co., 1971.

_____. *A Thomas Merton Reader*. Revised edition. Edited by Thomas P. McDonnell. New York: Image Books, 1974.

_____. *The Hidden Ground of Love: The Letters of Thomas Merton on Religious Experience and Social Concerns*. Selected and edited by William Shannon. New York: Farrar, Straus, Giroux, 1985.

_____. *The Inner Experience*. Published in *Cistercian Studies* Vol. XVIII (1983), I-IV and Vol. XIX (1984), V-VIII.

Griffin, John Howard. *A Hidden Wholeness: The Visual World of Thomas Merton*. Boston: Houghton Miflin Co., 1979.

Higgins, John. *Thomas Merton on Prayer*. New York: Image Books, 1975.

Mott, Michael. *The Seven Mountains of Thomas Merton*. Boston: Houghton Miflin, 1984.

*Thomas Merton, Monk. A Monastic Tribute*. Edited by Patrick Hart. New York: Sheed and Ward, 1974.

## C.S. LEWIS

Lewis, C.S. *Surprised By Joy*. London: Collins, Fontana Books, 1959.

_____. *Mere Christianity*. New York: Macmillan, 1960.

_____. *Letters to Malcolm: Chiefly on Prayer*. London: Collins, Fontana Books, 1966.

_____. *Reflections on the Psalms*. London: Collins, Fontana Books, 1958.

_____. *A Grief Observed*. New York: Seabury, 1961.

_____. *The Four Loves*. London: Collins, Fontana Books, 1960.

_____. *The Screwtape Letters.* New York: Macmillan, 1942.

_____. *The Problem of Pain.* London: Collins, Fontana Books, 1940.

_____. *Letters.* Edited by W.H. Lewis. New York: Harcourt, Brace, 1966.

_____. *Till We Have Faces: A Myth Retold.* Grand Rapids: Eerdmans, 1956.

Green, Roger Lancelyn, and Hooper, Walter. *C.S. Lewis, A Biography.* New York: Harcourt, Brace, Jovanovich, 1976.

Kilby, Clyde S. *The Christian World of C.S. Lewis.* Grand Rapids: Eerdmans, 1964.

Gibb, Jocelyn (editor). *Light on C.S. Lewis.* New York: Harcourt, Brace, 1965.

Kreeft, Peter. *C.S. Lewis: A Critical Essay.* Grand Rapids: Eerdmans, 1969.

## PIERRE TEILHARD DE CHARDIN

Teilhard de Chardin, Pierre. *The Divine Milieu.* New York: Harper and Row, 1960.

_____. *The Phenomenon of Man.* New York: Harper and Row, 1959.

_____. *The Future of Man.* New York: Harper and Row, 1964.

_____. *Hymn of the Universe.* New York: Harper and Row, 1965.

_____. *Writings in Time of War.* New York: Harper and Row, 1968.

_____. *Christianity and Evolution.* New York: Harcourt Brace Jovanovich, 1971.

Faricy, Robert. *Teilhard de Chardin's Theology of the Christian in the World.* New York: Sheed and Ward, 1967.

_____. *The Spirituality of Teilhard de Chardin.* Minneapolis: Winston Press, 1981.

Corbishley, Thomas. *The Spirituality of Teilhard de Chardin*. London: Collins, Fontana, 1971.

DeLubac, Henri. *The Religion of Teilhard de Chardin*. New York: Image Books, 1968.

Mooney, Christopher F. *Teilhard de Chardin and the Mystery of Christ*. New York: Image Books, 1968.


## CARYLL HOUSELANDER

Houselander, Caryll. *A Rocking-Horse Catholic*. New York: Sheed and Ward, 1955.

——————. *This War Is the Passion*. New York: Sheed and Ward, 1941.

——————. *The Reed of God*. New York: Sheed and Ward, 1944.

——————. *The Comforting of Christ*. New York: Sheed and Ward, 1947.

——————. *The Passion of the Infant Christ*. New York: Sheed and Ward, 1953.

——————. *The Risen Christ*. New York: Sheed and Ward, 1958.

——————. *Guilt*. New York: Sheed and Ward, 1951.

——————. "Christ in Men." *Integrity* (Sept., 1952), pp. 2-9.

——————. *Letters of Caryll Houselander*. Edited by Maisie Ward. New York: Sheed and Ward, 1965.

Ward, Maisie. *Caryll Houselander, The Divine Eccentric*. New York: Sheed and Ward, 1962.


## DIETRICH BONHOEFFER

Bonhoeffer, Dietrich. *The Cost of Discipleship*. New York: Macmillan, 1963.

_____. *Life Together*. New York: Harper and Row, 1954.
_____. *Letters and Papers from Prison*. Edited by Eberhard Bethge. New York: Macmillan, 1962.
_____. *Ethics*. New York: Macmillàn, 1965.
_____. *Christ the Center*. New York: Harper and Row, 1966.
Bethge, Eberhard. *Dietrich Bonhoeffer, Man of Vision, Man of Courage*. New York: Harper and Row, 1970.
Bosanquet, Mary. *The Life and Death of Dietrich Bonhoeffer*. New York: Harper and Row, 1968.


## COLUMBA MARMION

Marmion, Columba. *Christ the Life of the Soul*. St. Louis: Herder, 1925.
_____. *Christ in His Mysteries*. St. Louis: Herder, 1939.
_____. *Christ the Ideal of the Monk*. St. Louis: Herder, 1926.
_____. *Christ the Ideal of the Priest*. St. Louis: Herder, 1952.
_____. *Sponsa Verbi*. St. Louis: Herder, 1926.
_____. *The English Letters of Dom Marmion*. Baltimore: Helicon Press, 1962.
Thibaut, Dom Raymond. *Columba Marmion, A Master of the Spiritual Life*. London: Sands and Co., 1932.
Philipon, M.M. *The Spiritual Doctrine of Dom Marmion*. Westminster. MD: Newman Press, 1956.
*Abbot Marmion, An Irish Tribute*. Edited by the monks of Glenstal. Cork: Mercier Press, 1948.


## JOHN HENRY NEWMAN

Newman, John Henry. *Parochial and Plain Sermons*. 8 vols. London: Longmans, Green and Co., 1843. (These sermons have been frequently republished, most recently in a single volume edition by Ignatius Press, New York).

_____. *Sermons Preached on Various Occasions*. London: Longmans, Green and Co., 1900.

_____. *Discourses Addressed to Mixed Congregations*. Westminster, MD: Christian Classics, 1966.

_____. *Sermons on the Subjects of the Day*. London: Longmans, Green and Co., 1891.

_____. *Sermons Preached Before the University of Oxford*. London: Longmans, Green and Co., 1918.

_____. *Autobiographical Writings*. Edited with introductions by Henry Tristram. New York: Sheed and Ward, 1957.

_____. *Apologia Pro Vita Sua*. New York: Image Books, 1956.

_____. *Meditations and Devotions*. Westminster, MD: Christian Classics, 1975.

_____. *Realizations. Newman's Selection of His Parochial and Plain Sermons*. Edited with an introduction by Vincent Ferrer Blehl, S.J. London: Darton, Longman and Todd, 1964.

Bouyer, Louis. *Newman: His Life and Spirituality*. New York: P.J. Kennedy, 1958.

Graef, Hilda. *God and Myself: The Spirituality of John Henry Newman*. New York: Hawthorn Books, 1968.

Lamm, William. *The Spiritual Legacy of Newman*. Milwaukee: Bruce, 1934.

Trevor, Meriol. *Newman, The Pillar of the Cloud*. New York: Doubleday, 1962.

_____. *Newman, Light in Winter*. New York: Doubleday, 1962.